BREAK THE BUSINESS:

DECLARING YOUR INDEPENDENCE AND

ACHIEVING TRUE SUCCESS IN THE MUSIC INDUSTRY

BREAK THE BUSINESS:

DECLARING YOUR INDEPENDENCE AND

ACHIEVING TRUE SUCCESS IN THE MUSIC INDUSTRY

By: Ryan Kairalla

Printed in the United States.

First Printing, 2016

Title: Break the Business: Declaring Your Independence and
         Achieving True Success in the Music Industry
Registration No.: TXu001949506 / 2014-12-21
Author: Kairalla, Ryan Andrew
Publisher: Corey/Klock Books
            555 Washington Ave. Suite 310
            Miami Beach, Florida 33139
Editor: Peter J. Klock, II
Foreword: Bill "Spruke" Boulden
Afterword: Josh Morales, Esq.

ISBN-13: 978-0692590669

First Edition

For Qiuying.

你是一個天使

Acknowledgements

Many truly wonderful people supported me throughout this endeavor, and I am immeasurably grateful to each and every one of them. Thank you to:

Mom (the strongest person I know), Dad, Lauren Kairalla (for all of your support), Jason Kairalla, Stephen Kairalla, Elisha Kairalla, Jennifer Kairalla, my dear Qiuying, my outstanding nieces and nephews, my grandparents, my cousins, my uncles and aunts, the Corey Klock Books/Corey Consulting team (Chris, Brian, Peter, Elsie, Richard, and the rest!), Melanie Garcia, Bill Teck, Eric Martinez, David Kaye, Bill Boulden, Mary Jennings (for all that you have done), Eric Sussman, C.T. Fields, Natalie Gelman, Kim Boekbinder, Meri Amber, J.P. Kallio, Josh Morales, Elizabeth Morales, Elisa Melendez, Evan Lamb, J.C. Smith, Alex Privee, Fernando Zulueta, Tom Muzquiz, Academica, Academica Virtual Education, the faculty and staff at Doral College, my students, my clients, and most of all...the thousands upon thousands of talented, entrepreneurial, and innovative independent musicians out there whose courage and work product inspire all of us. These musicians are the new industry. They are breaking the models of old and putting the creators in control—much to the benefit of music fans.

IMPORTANT NOTICE

The information presented in this book represents the opinions of the author on the subjects discussed and may not apply to all situations. The book's contents and the views of its author are presented for informational and entertainment purposes only and do not constitute legal advice. Though every effort was made to ensure that the contents of this book were accurate and current as of the time of this writing, laws, facts, and industry norms can change over time and information presented in this book might be out of date even by the time the book was first published. The author and the publisher assume no responsibility for any actions taken by readers based on the advice offered in this book. Readers should proceed with the utmost caution in applying any of the materials in this book to their specific circumstances, and should retain the services and seek the advice of an attorney or other appropriate professional when making career decisions. A book is not a substitute for seeking the counsel of a relevant professional. Every person's legal or business issues are unique. While information in this book might bear similarities to a reader's situation, only through receiving a relevant professional's guidance can a person make fully-informed decisions regarding their particular legal or business needs.

CONTENTS

FOREWORD

There's a psychological/storytelling concept known as the "Princess Fantasy." The Princess Fantasy explains part of the appeal of Disney films, and children's fascination with princesses. A huge part of it is the *value* and *meaning* being a princess imparts to life's otherwise mundane activities. When a princess wants to walk in a garden, a beautiful garden, meticulously tended, is always awaiting her. And people appear to watch, and compliment her in hushed whispers, as she walks it. If a princess decides she's eligible for dating, suitors magically appear in a jostling line. If a princess sings a song, *the animals sing along and already know all the words.* Everybody knows the princess' song, because she's the main character! It is an attractive and pervasive fantasy.

Now think of the typical Band Movie where the protagonist signs a record deal and instantly makes it big. Do you recognize some similarities? Please ask yourself, is the place where you imagine your music career heading nothing more than a Princess Fantasy?

Welcome to Ryan Kairalla's book, *Break the Business.* He gets it. He understands why the Princess Fantasy has so much staying power in our consciousness, even though he's seen it repeatedly take advantage of, screw over, and ruin artist after artist. He's here to save you from it. Listen to what he has to say. He's got a workable alternative for you, and he's funny as hell as he walks you through it, too.

I'm Spruke, or Bill Boulden if you're addressing me in

human form. You may not have heard of me, but I'm "minor-niche famous." As this is the only kind of "famous" that's really accessible to us muggles anymore, if you're reading this book, hopefully it's in store for you as well. If you're a board-game geek or competitive collectible card game player who also likes EDM, it's very likely you know who I am. If you listen to the radio in your car, you'll never have heard of me. Let me tell you a little about my music career.

In 2015, seventeen years after I recorded my first song, thirteen years after I released my first EP album in print, eight years after I released my first LP digitally, three years after starting to produce my weekly *Bump In The Night* Podcast, eight months after prewriting four-fifths of an entire album without sharing it with anybody, and two weeks after learning to produce my own videos: **I finally turned a profit.**

I wish I'd had this book about eight years ago when I started seriously pushing my music online. I wasted so much effort, so much energy, and so much money trying and failing using the "conventional" methods that Ryan warns us all about before I wised up and started doing things The Indie Way.

The record companies' business model revolves around taking hundreds of thousands of wannabe princesses, turning two to three per year into actual princesses, and dashing the hopes of the rest upon the rocks while extracting any value they can for themselves. The lack of good information about the realities of the music industry, combined with the perception that record companies are the gatekeepers to that fantasy life, has allowed labels to profit off the dreams of thousands of starry-eyed hopefuls by telling them they'll be the next big thing if they just sign that dotted line.

But guess what? The record companies aren't actually the gatekeepers to the entertainment industry anymore. The actual gatekeeper now is the **hustle**. Will you sign your name to the hustle? The terms of that agreement are in this book. You'll find them far more agreeable than the terms the record labels are proposing. And it's a contract that your new entertainment lawyer friend—Ryan—will advise you to go ahead and sign.

Your deal with the hustle won't be easy. In fact, you might make music for seventeen years, print physical albums for thirteen, put your music in stores digitally for eight, produce an hour-long piece of content every week to give away freely for three, and teach yourself more about video production than you ever knew about audio production, before your lifetime balance finally winds up in the black. But, if you employ the lessons you'll learn, *Break the Business* will help you stand a much greater chance at success.

I'll see you there.

-Bill "Spruke" Boulden

PART I

WHY YOU DON'T WANT A RECORD LABEL

CHAPTER 1
INTRODUCTION

Congratulations!

You have worked very hard, you have had some great early success in life, and now you're finally ready to buy your first house. But you're a bit of a free spirit, and you don't want to live in some cookie-cutter dwelling that looks like every other place on the block. You want to *build* your own house, and live in something that's truly special and unique.

A large bank has heard about your interest in homebuilding and has an intriguing offer for you to consider: The bank will loan you money to build your dream house, but only under certain conditions. First, to pay off the loan, you will have to give a large portion of your income each month to the bank, but only a small percentage of that money will actually go toward paying off your balance. Moreover, even though you have a very specific vision for what you want your house to look like, and you happen to be quite skilled at architecture, the bank still gets to make all final decisions on every aspect of the house's design and construction.

But wait, there's more: Once your house is built, the bank can (and most likely will) force you to build more houses for them under the same lending terms, even if you don't want to build those houses. Even if you believe that there are better uses for your time and labor, you will be stuck. And you have to keep taking the same large loans from them to build those houses. And as you finish each house, the bank will continue to take a large portion of your income, and will keep doing so until the balances on *all* of your home loans are paid off. This will take a very long time, if it happens at all because, as previously noted, only a small percentage of what you pay actually goes toward paying off your debt.

Oh, and whether you pay off the loans or not, the bank gets to keep every single one of the houses you built. You heard that right: *They* own all of *your* houses. Fully and completely.

Does this sound like a good deal to you?

If not, then stay the hell away from record contracts, because if you change "house" to "album" in the example above, then those are basically the terms of a standard deal with a typical record label.

◆ ◆ ◆

If you are reading this book, you're probably interested in a career in the music industry. You want to be a big star and make a big impact on the world, and I think that's wonderful. I happen to love musicians and have many musician friends. They are my favorite kind of people. In fact, the very reason I went to law school and became an entertainment lawyer was so that I could help creative souls just like you share their gifts with the world. I admire you because of your unyielding desire to pursue your dreams even though so many people in your life (including your own family, most likely) probably told you to give up at some point.

Have I buttered you up enough? Good.

Because I also want to tell you, in case you didn't already know, that the odds are ridiculously stacked against you. Achieving high levels of success as a musician is *really* tough. To have even a small chance of breaking through, you have to work harder and have more talent than the top one percent of the top one percent. There are basically three job openings for "International Music Sensation" right now and a bazillion qualified applicants who want the position. I don't care how skilled you are (although I'm sure that you are *amazing*); I would sooner bet on you meeting a leprechaun, while riding a talking unicorn to a Beatles reunion concert, than bet on you "making it" in this industry.

That being said, follow your dreams. I believe in you! Did I mention that I love musicians?

What this Book Won't Do

Because there are so many of you vying for this brass ring, you will find no shortage of books out there geared toward giving musicians advice on breaking into the industry. Many of these "how to" books are centered around landing a coveted "record deal" to achieve success—as if the mere act of signing your name on a label contract will immediately bring you great fortune and cause Grammy awards to descend from the sky.

4

Let me absolve you of this notion now. Getting "signed" will not necessarily bring you long-term success in the music industry. If you need proof of this, go to the website of any major label and look at their full roster of artists. After you get past the handful of genuine superstars, you'll find yourself saying "Who the hell is that?" at roughly half of the names on the list, and "That band still exists?!?" at the other half.

Despite all of this, those music business books devote page after page to suggesting supposedly fast and easy routes to getting a record deal. This book will not do that. If you are looking for the "how to get signed" book, then keep looking. Or, better yet, let me save you nineteen bucks and just summarize those books for you in a hundred words or less: If you want a record deal (according to those how-to guides), just:

1) Record a demo tape with a couple rough recordings on it,
2) make a press kit featuring your photos and a biography (preferably, dripping with hyperbole),
3) get an entertainment lawyer to "shop" your demo and press kit to record companies,
4) sign a record deal, and, finally,
5) do the backstroke in the solid gold pool filled with the money you just earned.

Cheekiness aside, the "advice" from those books is outdated at best and pure nonsense at worst. First of all, the days of getting "discovered" with a rough demo tape you recorded in your parents' basement are long gone. Today, many labels expect you to come to them with a completely finished album—and a pretty decent following of fans—before they will even consider taking you on. And having a lawyer "shop" your music to labels? Come on, that's just silly. Do you really think you're going to get a "yes" from an A&R department just because some tone-deaf shyster vouches for your talent? Take it from this tone-deaf shyster: Record deals don't happen that way anymore. Labels don't care about what people like me think.

What This Book Will Do

So, no, this book will not help you get signed. Instead, it will give you far more valuable advice. Rather than help you get closer to labels, this book will outline the reasons why you need to stay far, far away from them. Rather than suggest ways to get you into "the business," the ensuing chapters will instruct you on how to be your *own* business. Setting out to be your own business is the most important thing musicians can do nowadays, because not only is a record contract extremely unlikely to result in your superstardom, but signing one also poses a significant risk of completely ruining your life—as it has for many of my friends and clients.

If you have never read one before, a standard record contract is a very long and complicated document. The lengthiest ones can easily be over 100 pages. They are a bewildering mass of oddly-defined terms, industry jargon, counter-intuitive clauses, and lawyerly gobbledygook. Often, seasoned entertainment lawyers will have to spend many hours sifting through them to even begin to comprehend the terms of such an agreement. And any lawyer who ever claims to *fully* understand the terms and risks of a particular contract is either lying or ignorant. Record contracts are a mess, and that is exactly how record companies like it. Purposefully buried within that indecipherable stack of papers is a collection of clauses designed specifically to rob artists blind and to continue robbing them blind for years to come.

The rest of the chapters in this part of the book will break down a standard record deal and show you just how nasty these agreements can be. Granted, not every record deal will have all of the terms I will describe, but the vast majority of them do. In fact, the contractual terms I will discuss in the subsequent chapters are so entrenched in the industry that it is all but impossible for lawyers like me to negotiate any of them away on your behalf. Labels come into the transaction with little inclination to change the way they do things, and the least-friendly terms in the contract are usually presented as a take-it-or-leave-it scenario for the artist.

Unless you want your music career to end up like your hypothetical homebuilding career that we previously discussed, I suggest you choose the latter.

CHAPTER 2

YOU WILL PAY FOR THIS RECORD DEAL

The Talk

It is an unfortunate fact that many early-career artists who sign record deals do so without the advice and assistance of counsel. Entertainment lawyers are expensive, and struggling musicians understandably bristle at springing for a lawyer when doing so would cut into their "eating to survive" budget. So they do without, and they hope that they are not making a perilous and life-destroying decision in the process (Spoiler alert: They are.).

But every once in a while, an artist is fortunate enough to get a legal professional involved before they sign their name to anything. Maybe the artist was making some decent coin playing live shows and could scrape together a retainer. Or maybe the artist was able to get some free advice from a lawyer in her family who was sufficiently guilted into helping out a fellow relative. Many lawyers I know have been called upon to help a family member in need. Once you get your law license, it's amazing how many eighth-cousins-thrice-removed come out of the woodwork seeking uncompensated counsel.

When it comes to entertainment advice, however, I am usually willing to provide free legal services to most family members, friends, and friends-of-friends who need it. As I noted in the previous chapter, I became a lawyer specifically to help musicians. I knew damn well when I started that most musicians tend not to rank amongst the well to do (not when they first start their careers, at least). If I restricted myself to assisting only musicians with money, I would be awfully short on people to help.

Besides, when a musician comes to me with a record contract and wants my advice for free, I have my own unique form of compensation: Before I do any work, they have to let me give them "The Talk" first.

The Talk is my long-winded and sermonizing lecture for why they should not sign this deal that they have worked their whole life to earn. I go through all of the troublesome terms of these agreements in excruciating detail. The Talk tends to drag on for quite a while, and has only increased in length over my young career as I read through one soul-crushing record contract after another. By the end of The Talk, I have usually annoyed and disenchanted my client so much that they wish they had simply paid me when they had the chance.

Toward the end of The Talk, I usually switch from a droning oration to more of a question-and-answer format in the hope that some back-and-forth discussion might get my increasingly impatient client to change their mind about signing. The conversation usually goes something like this:

"Why do you even *want* to work with a record company?" I inquire.

"They will record my music and put it in stores so that people can buy it," they inevitably respond.

"You don't need a record company for that," I reply. "These days, record companies don't record your albums anyway. You will most likely be the one that has to manage the actual recording. And there are plenty of companies out there who will put your music on iTunes, on music streaming services, and in stores for next to nothing. Why would you need a label for that sort of thing?"

After being momentarily taken aback, my client will usually point out: "But what about marketing and promotion? The record label probably has a huge marketing department that will advertise my music."

Which prompts my ready response: "Actually, you might be surprised to know that nothing in the contract even *obligates* the label to do any promotion for you. They can just sit on the record if they want to and leave you to promote the album with no support. Moreover, most of the promotion done by labels is not done in-house anymore. To the extent that they feel like doing any promotion on your record, they will usually contract with independent promoters to do it. So if what you really want is someone to promote your music, why use a label at all? Why not just contract with those independent promoters yourself?"

My client retorts with little hesitation. "I can't pay for that stuff! I need a label to buy those things for me. I'm not a millionaire lawyer like you," he says to the guy with $185 in his bank account and six figures of student loan debt.

It is at this point that I drop the hammer. "Well, here's the thing about that. Under this contract, *you* pay for all of those things. Not the label. In fact, you pay for pretty much everything."

"What?" My client responds, somewhat confused. "No, no, no. That can't be right. The deal is that I contribute my labor to make the record, and the label contributes their money to sell the record. That *has* to be how it works, right?"

"Wrong. *You* make the record, and *you* pay for it."

My client will usually pause as this information sinks in, and his face will contort like he smells something rotten. Then, suddenly, he'll blurt out, "Well, what in the hell does the label do?"

Get Ready To Pay Up

The shock that musicians have when I give them that particular piece of information is certainly understandable. For one thing, they usually come to me believing that the record contract in their hand represents a desire by a label to make a real investment in their career. They thought that the record company would be putting some skin in the game. When I tell them that this is not really the case, that in fact it is the artist that shoulders the true financial burden of their record deal, it is more than a little disconcerting to them.

The second reason why my little revelation catches them by surprise is that none of what I tell them is immediately apparent when you read a standard recording agreement. You will not find an "ARTIST hereby agrees to pay for everything" clause clearly spelled out in the contract. In fact, the contract will even feature some language stating how the label will pay the recording costs of the artist's albums and may even cover some of the album's promotion expenses.

That would seem to completely contradict everything that I just told my client. So, what gives? Rest assured, the "Artist pays for everything" language is very much a part of standard record contracts; the language is just buried quite well. After all, if you're a label in the business of profiting off musicians' backs, it helps to conceal your tactics a bit.

The Recording Process

To understand how a record contract imposes a financial burden on the artist, you have to understand the process by which an album gets made under a recording agreement. You might feel like you know something about how the recording process works, particularly if you've seen movies like *Ray, Rock Star, or Dreamgirls.* Those movies will usually show some kind of recording session scene or montage taking place in a label's studio. The scene is a well-worn film trope: It starts with a nameless studio technician pointing to the artist-protagonist on the other side of a glass partition, signaling to the artist that the recording has begun. The band starts to play together, and they nail the song perfectly on the first try, because they are the heroes of the story and heroes don't need two takes. All the while, the camera pans to a couple of label executives sitting in the control room, smiling and patting each other on the back because they *know* that they just heard the next big hit.

Like many things presented to us by Hollywood, these scenes are wildly inaccurate. For one thing, high-quality music recordings are never produced perfectly and simultaneously in one take. In fact, each instrument is usually recorded separately for ease of editing. Many takes for each instrument are usually required. And, after the standard band instruments are recorded, some additional instruments and other "sweeteners" will be overdubbed to create a richer sound. Then, someone has to edit and comp the whole thing. This process typically involves some poor engineer pondering his life choices while he spends eight hours repeatedly listening to the same seven seconds of playback until he can get the sound to come out just right—or until he kills himself—whichever comes first.

The trope of the smiling label executives in the company studio is also quite fictional. The vast majority of recording studios these days are not label-owned, and executives are usually nowhere to be found in most recording sessions. Instead, studios tend to be independently owned and located in crappy neighborhoods where industry suits fear to tread. In fact, most artists are usually surprised to find out how little involvement record companies tend to have with the making of the actual record. After the label approves the song choices and sets the recording budget, the record contract tasks

10

the artist with doing everything else required to deliver a finished album to the label. Sometimes, the artist is even responsible for doing the requisite menial paperwork to make the album, such as preparing all of the tax, immigration, and union forms for all of the participants in the recording process. Given most musicians' extensive background in tax, immigration, and labor law, this is *obviously* no problem for them.

But let's put that little annoyance aside for a moment and get back to the main issue: who *pays* for your masterpiece to be recorded. The record contract usually provides for the handling of recording costs in one of two ways. Either the label will cover the expenses outlined in the approved recording budget, or it will pay a "recording fund" to the artist and the artist will pay the recording costs out of that fund.

The Soul-Crushing Terror That Is Recoupment

So far, the funding process for an album seems quite equitable, doesn't it? The artist supplies the labor and the label supplies the capital. Sounds fair. It seems conceivable that what would happen next is that the sales from the album would then be split in some way to compensate each side for what they contributed to the project. The artist would get a chunk for their investment of time and labor, and the label would get a chunk for their investment of money. And if enough albums are sold, then both sides profit from their investment. That's totally how it works, right?

Not a chance. If it worked that way, I wouldn't be writing this book. You see, the scenario I just described would be an example of a *fair* business deal—one in which the artist was not getting turbo-screwed by his or her label. Instead, standard record deals state that the artist does not receive any "royalties" (i.e., the artist's cut of record sales) until the label makes back every dollar of what it spent on recording costs. This is known as "recoupment." Once that wrinkle gets added to the mix, the business arrangement starts to look a little more one-sided. Recoupment allows the label to start feeding at the trough long before the artist does. The artist does not get so much as a nibble for their work until the label makes its recording investment back.

11

And if you think that is unfair, wait until you hear the best part. Record contracts also stipulate that the label recoups its recording costs *solely* from the artist's royalties. Wrap your head around what this means. Before the artist gets any money from sales of the music, the label gets to recoup recording costs not from *all* of the money made, but just from the *artist's share* of the money. And, because the artist's share of the royalties is a pittance, the album generally has to be a smash hit in order for the artist's royalties to get over the recoupment hurdle and finally start making their way to the artist's pocket. We'll get into the details of what an artist can expect their share of the royalties to be in Chapter 4, but, for the moment, just take it on faith that it ain't much.

One implication of this is that it will take a much longer time for the artist to see any royalties, because the label is using a smaller pool of money to recoup its investment. Another implication is that the label's "investment" in the artist is actually not an investment at all. Let's call it what it really is: It is a loan, pure and simple (and a loan with horrifyingly bad terms, at that). The record company is the bank, and the artist is its debtor.

The artist will pay back that loan from the money to which they are otherwise entitled under the contract. Thus, record deals require artists to shoulder the complete financial burden of making a record, just as they would if they'd made it themselves. The only difference is that, with a record deal, the artist gets a much smaller piece of the revenues generated by the record than if they had simply stayed independent.

To make matters worse (as if they weren't bad enough already) the label's recouping party does not stop at the recording costs. In fact, record contracts usually stipulate that nearly *every* significant expense the record company incurs with regard to your album will be paid back out of your royalties. The recoupable costs frequently include:

- Nonstandard album design, packaging, and manufacturing costs
- Costs of producing and releasing music videos to promote your album
- Costs of paying independent promoters for your album

- Independent marketing expenses for your album
- Costs of presenting any live promotional performances of your music
- Costs pertaining to the use of your recordings on mobile devices (e.g., creating ringtones, ringbacks, and mobile artwork)
- Costs associated with your website (e.g., design, hosting, and maintenance)

Basically, the label gets to recoup damn near everything that relates to the album from your royalties. I repeat: You are on the hook for everything. Record deal or no record deal, it is the artist who pays for costs pertaining to the creation, promotion, and sale of the album. Granted, it was not always this way. Labels used to rightfully see many of these expenditures as a "cost of doing business" for them, and did not try to foist those debts upon artists. Unfortunately, these more scrupulous practices are those of a bygone era, and they have long since joined leg warmers and parachute pants as footnotes in history. Nowadays, the label might flash its credit card at first, but ultimately it is the artist who gets stuck with the bill.

In conclusion, whether you sign your name to a record contract or not, you will pay for your album and the accompanying costs required to sell it. So why sign that contract? If the costs are yours either way, why let someone else keep the lion's share of the benefits?

CHAPTER 3

YOU DO NOT OWN YOUR RECORDINGS

A Nasty Loan

So far, our analysis of a typical record deal has revealed a rather unpleasant business transaction for the artist. In this transaction, the artist and label agree to have the artist do the work to create an album while also bearing the ultimate financial responsibility for the creation, marketing, promotion, and other costs associated with the album. In this transaction, the label acts as a very unusual bank. The label essentially "loans" the money to the artist for the album's costs. In return for the loan, the label gets paid back from the artist's royalties and, on top of that, gets to keep the vast majority of the proceeds from the album's sales. This is a sweet deal for the label, but not so sweet for the artist.

Given the way I describe the arrangement, some might say I am being a too hard on the labels. Even if a record company is nothing more than a bank, minus the friendly tellers and lollypops for visiting children, so what? What's so bad about banks? Is it necessarily evil to be a lending institution?

Of course not. Generally, I have no problem with what banks do. Debt financing is often an effective means for people to move their lives forward. Without the lending provided by banks, it would be impossible for most people to attend college, start a business, or own a home.

Some of the most valuable things we get in life, we get through loans. So why should an album be any different? For example, if I want to start my own restaurant, going to a bank for financing would likely be a prudent means to accomplish that goal. Moreover, it would be perfectly reasonable for the bank to expect me to pay them back at some point. In that same vein, if I was a musician and wanted to make my own album for sale, what is wrong with a record company loaning me money to make that happen?

Nothing is wrong with it, in theory. But the problem with record labels is that the terms of their "loans" are so one-sided that signing on the dotted line will get the borrower into a world of trouble. In the next few chapters, you will see how a lot of the clauses in a record contract make these particular loans a bad move on your part, both financially and professionally. But for now, I will share the fundamental difference between most typical loans (for things like houses, cars, and businesses) and the loans offered by record companies: With typical loans, you actually *get* something.

When you take out a mortgage, and then pay it off, you own a house free and clear. When you finance a car, you make each excruciating monthly payment because there's a four-wheeled piece of collateral that you would like to keep in your driveway. And when you make your final payment on that sixtieth month, that car is yours to keep. Paying off loans sucks, but we do it because it is often the only way for us to own expensive things. But when you take a record label's "loan" to make an album, you don't keep the album. The label does.

Basically, in a record deal, the label gets to keep your loan payments, and it gets to keep the collateral. This would be akin to a bank owning your house regardless of whether or not you paid off your mortgage. As explained in the previous chapter, the artist bears the ultimate financial responsibility for the albums created under a record contract. But in this case, paying for the album does not mean the artist gets to own the album. In fact, it is just the opposite. Recordings created under a record contract are the property of the record label, despite the fact that the artist effectively pays for those recordings.

An Introduction to Copyright

Before we get any further into this discussion, it would be helpful to explain what I mean by "property" when it comes to albums. When I say "property" in this context, I don't mean it in the physical sense. I am not talking about ownership of the physical copies of the albums themselves. Each physical copy (or digital copy, as the case may be) of an album is owned by whichever consumer chooses to purchase that copy from a brick-and-mortar store or off the Internet. The property to which I am referring in this discussion is the "intellectual property" of an album, otherwise known as the album's copyright. This "property" is much more valuable than the individual copies.

In the music industry, owning the copyright on an album is known as owning the "master rights" of an album. Master rights are the copyright in the recording of each song on an album. Owning the master rights and owning a song are not the same thing; the master is just a particular recorded version of a song. For example, the copyright to the song "White Christmas" (i.e., the music and lyrics themselves) is owned by the Irving Berlin Music Company. However, that musical composition has been recorded by many different artists, including recent hitmakers like Taylor Swift and Lady Gaga. Each one of those recordings has separate master rights, which are likely owned by those artists' respective record companies.

To see why album copyrights matter, you need to know what a copyright is and what makes them so valuable. In the United States, our copyright law comes from a system of federal legal protections for "creative works." The creative works protected by copyright law include almost any artistic endeavor you can think of, such as books, musical compositions, plays, photographs, paintings, movies, television shows, sound recordings (including musical sound recordings), architectural blueprints and renderings, and much more.

Getting Copyright Protection

For something to receive copyright protection, the law imposes two very simple requirements. First, the work must be sufficiently "original." Recent cases have set the originality bar quite low, with the Supreme Court holding that a work need only have a "modicum of creativity" to meet this requirement. Basically, if you scribbled a drawing of a clown onto a cocktail napkin, that drawing could very well be original enough for copyright protection. The second requirement is that your creative-enough work has to be "fixed in a tangible medium of expression." This is just fancy lawyer-talk for the work having to be embodied in some permanent way. For example, the moment that a story is written down on a sheet of paper (or saved on a computer), a movie is recorded on film, a song is sung onto a tape recorder (or digitally recorded), or, for that matter, your clown is drawn on the cocktail napkin, that particular creative work has copyright protection.

16

Some of my musician clients are often surprised when I share this information with them. When I tell them that obtaining a copyright is literally as simple as writing something on a piece of paper, they respond by saying a combination of:

"But I thought I had to register my song."

"Don't I need to publish my work first?"

"Don't I have to give copies of my work to the government?"

"Isn't there a fee I need to pay?"

"My friend told me I had to put my song in an envelope and mail it to myself.

And, my personal favorite, "But I need to put the funky-looking 'C' symbol with a circle around it on my work somewhere, right?"

Let me answer all of those questions in order: You don't, you don't, you don't, there isn't, save yourself the stamp because your friend is ridiculous, and no. By the way, that funky-looking "©" symbol is called a copyright notice. And while it is a useful thing to put on your copyrighted work to inform others of your intellectual property rights, it is not required by law anymore.

Many of the misconceptions that people have about obtaining a copyright persist for a number of reasons. Some of them are the product of old legal formality requirements that no longer exist in this country. Before the copyright laws were changed in 1976, unpublished works or works published without a proper copyright notice would not receive federal protection. Other misconceptions, such as registering your work for a fee and depositing copies with the Copyright Office, are also not required to create a copyright. That being said, following these formalities is generally a smart thing to do because, among other reasons, they establish when your work was created.

Copyright Registration

In fact, let's digress for a bit and talk about why copyright registration in particular is so important. Don't worry, we'll get back to "Why Record Deals are Dangerous" in just a moment. But since the ultimate purpose of this book is to help you further your music business ambitions, I think there's nothing wrong with sprinkling in some helpful information and general career advice along the way.

While it is not required to obtain a copyright, registering your works with the government provides you with a lot of valuable benefits that make doing it a good idea.

Here's an example to show why this is the case: Let's say you wrote an original song and recorded it onto a tape recorder (because you are an old soul). As we noted before, by doing that, you now have a copyright on your song. A few weeks later, one of your rival musicians (don't ask me why you have a rival; maybe you should try being nicer to people) gets a hold of your tape, hears your awesome song, and decides to re-record his own version without your permission and sell copies to all of his fans. Guess what? Your rival totally infringed on your copyright. This dastardly deed cannot go unpunished! Can you take this thief to court and get him to pay damages?

The answer to the question, "Can I sue?" is *always* "yes." The pertinent question, however, is, "Can I win?" Well, before you can get any money, you are going to have to prove that you are the original copyright holder. Good luck with that! Your rival has your tape, remember? Besides, even if you still had your recording, how are you going to prove that you recorded your version before he recorded his version (unless your recording has some sort of time stamp)?

One way you could have avoided this predicament is by registering your copyright once you created your little opus. Registration of your work not only gives you proof of the work's creation date, but courts will treat your registration as a presumption of your copyright ownership. Having this presumption in your favor means that you no longer have to prove you are the original copyright holder. Instead, the burden now lies with your copycat nemesis, who now must show, with evidence, that you are *not* the copyright holder. This makes it an uphill battle for the other guy, rather than for you.

And please, for the love of God, don't be one of those musicians who believes that mailing yourself a copy of your work for the postmark date and leaving the envelope sealed is just as good as getting a formal copyright registration. These so-called "poor man's copyrights" carry just about as much evidentiary weight as writing "Pretty Please!" on a sheet of paper and handing it to the jury. Don't do it! It is easy too easy to fake this type of evidence; envelopes can be steam-opened and postmark dates can be doctored, which basically renders this method of copyright protection useless. Conversely, doing it the right way and getting an official government registration will make you all but invincible. Besides, copyright registration is a relatively painless process anyway. You can register your work online using the Copyright Office's website in just a few minutes. The filing fees will only set you back $35, which is a small price to pay for nearly bulletproof protection.

Registration of your work has another benefit as well. If you register your work before an act of infringement occurs, then you will be entitled to "statutory damages" from the infringer. Statutory damages are a fixed sum that is pre-set by federal copyright law. These are the type of damages you want to seek, because you do not have to prove any specific dollar value of injury to get them. If you do not register your work before an infringement occurs, then you can only obtain the amount in damages that you can sufficiently demonstrate you suffered because of the infringer's actions. These are known as "actual damages," and they are often very hard to prove.

To help illustrate all of this, here's a famous real-life story (from outside of music) to show you what I mean. Back in 1995, the Cleveland Browns announced they were moving their franchise to Baltimore and changing their name to the Ravens. A Baltimore-area security guard named Fredrick Bouchat was so excited about getting a team in his hometown that he hand-drew a proposed logo for the new team and sent it to the Ravens, asking only for an autographed helmet and a letter of recognition should they decide to use his idea. Instead, the Ravens basically decided to steal his logo and give him nothing in return for it. In this case, the infringement was quite clear: The team's eventual logo looked almost exactly like Bouchat's drawing.

Unfortunately, Bouchat did not receive any damages at trial, despite the court's holding that the Ravens did indeed steal his design. You see, Bouchat had not registered the copyright before the infringement occurred, giving him no right to statutory damages. And any hopes he had for getting actual damages were basically dead in the water since there was no way he could precisely identify any damages he suffered or profits the team accrued from its use of his logo.

Moral of the story: If you write a good song, PLEASE register it! I do not want you to become the Frederick Bouchat of the music business.

Ok, my copyright registration digression is over. Let's get back to ripping on record labels again.

Why Are Copyrights Important?

Now that we have established how a work gets copyright protection, let's look at what a copyright gives its holder. The "property" embodied within a copyright is actually a series of rights to do things with your work that no one else can do but you (unless you give them permission, for which you can charge a fee). In other words, these rights are considered "exclusive" to the copyright holder (who, barring certain exceptions, is generally the person who created the work). One of these exclusive rights is in the name of the principle itself: A "copyright" gives you the exclusive right to make copies of your work. A copyright also lets you exclusively distribute (e.g., sell, lease, lend, etc.) your work, perform your work in public, display your work in public, and make new works based on your old work (which are known as "derivative works").

When you think about what these exclusive rights mean, one can see how having them can make you quite wealthy if you have created a great original work. For example, if you wrote a novel, this "bundle of rights," as they are commonly called, allows you to control who can make copies of your book, who can sell those copies to others, or who can make your book into a movie (which is one example of a derivative work). If you control these rights, no one is allowed to do these things with your work unless you give them a "license" to do so. And if your work is good, people might be willing to pay you big bucks for those licenses (think of J.K. Rowling's *Harry Potter* series, and the movies and merchandise that followed, all of which she profited from because she maintained ownership of her copyrights).

Similarly, if you have a copyright on an album you made, you can make copies of that album and sell it to others. You can also license the right to play tracks from your album to satellite radio stations or to Internet streaming stations like Pandora, Spotify, Apple Music, or Rdio. You can license your recordings to be in compilation albums, or even put your music in commercials, TV shows, and movies. The avenues available to monetize your recordings are seemingly infinite. And as the copyright holder, those things can only happen with your permission—permission that you can readily sell to others for the right price.

Your Work Is Not Your Work

But before you get too excited about all of these potential income opportunities, do not forget the main point of this chapter. NONE of this applies to you if you are making recorded music under a standard record deal. As stated earlier, if there is a record contract involved, the *record company* owns the master rights—not you. Consequently, they get to control, and profit from, everything that is done with those master rights. Sure, the contract will have some provisions that give you a piece of the money they make (such as your sales royalties), but that's all you get: a piece of the pie (and a sliver, at that). The rest of the pie—the pie that you baked, by the way—is theirs.

Works For Hire

The more perceptive readers might have noted something inconsistent between the above paragraph and something I said earlier about copyrights. I previously noted that copyrights generally belong to whoever created the work in question. This is indeed the law. If you write a story, you own that story. If you paint a portrait, you own the rights to that portrait. So if the artist is the person who makes the album under a record deal, how come they do not own any of the rights in the deal? What makes albums different?

The record contract does. Record contracts almost always have a clause that deems new albums a "work for hire." Works for hire are an exception to the general "author is the owner" rule in American copyright law. It allows someone other than the creator of a work to become the owner of the copyright. In this case, the album would be a work for hire for the label, meaning they get to own your master rights. You, conversely, own nothing.

Work for hire situations tend to come up most often in the employer-employee context as a means for a large organization to create massive amounts of content. For example, let's say that you worked as an animator for a TV cartoon show. Every week at your job, you would probably draw hundreds of pictures for the program. Since you drew those pictures, does that mean you own the copyrights? Not a chance. Before you picked up your sketch pad on the first day of work, the production company had you sign a contract saying that everything you draw for the show is a work for hire. This means that everything you draw at their direction (and often anything you draw using their tools or materials) belongs to them.

Is there something unethical or wrong about this company getting to own your creations? Actually, no. For one thing, this process represents the most effective way for the production company to make its TV show. The company has many animators on staff and needs to be able to efficiently combine all of their works together to create the final product. This can be done with greater ease if the production company owns the rights to all of the drawings instead of each individual animator controlling their respective drawings. And despite the fact that each animator is giving up rights to their creations, the deal is still a fair one for the artist. As employees of the production company, all of the animators are receiving a salary and benefits in exchange for the intellectual property they create on the job. It is a reasonable trade.

When content creators are employees of a larger organization and creating parts of a larger whole (like individual drawings for a cartoon show), work for hire arrangements make perfect sense. Moreover, the business transaction is reasonably equitable for everyone involved. But in the world of record contracts, the work for hire model becomes less a means for efficient content creation and more a vehicle for exploiting artists. Unlike our cartoon show example, the album created by the artist is not part of some larger whole that needs to be easily combined with other things to create a final product. The album *is* the final product. Thus, making the album a work for hire serves no functional purpose other than making the label richer and the artist poorer.

Record companies do not *need* to have the master rights to accomplish the goals of a record deal. Instead, the contract could keep the artist in control of their copyrights and have the artist simply give the record company a license to sell and otherwise exploit the work. This is the practice in many book publishing deals (at least the fair ones, anyway). Record labels could certainly do the same thing in their contracts. In fact, when dealing with their more famous artists (who have more power at the negotiating table due to that fame), labels often do have such deals. They just don't want to do it with you. They want to keep your stuff and they know that you have no leverage to stop them.

The second injustice with having a work for hire clause in a record contract is that there is no employer-employee relationship between the label and the artist. In the cartoon show example, you gave up your intellectual property rights in exchange for being a salaried employee. But in the case of a record deal, you are not the label's employee and are entitled to none of the benefits that come with that role. The label is not giving you a paycheck every two weeks. There's no record company health plan being offered to you. The only things you are getting from the label are royalties, which are, of course, earmarked to pay for the costs of your album before you get a single penny.

If you record a great album, your master rights could potentially be worth millions. When a label offers you a contract, not only are they trying to get those millions for next to nothing, they are not even going to pay for the album in exchange for getting those millions. Don't let them anywhere near your intellectual property; it is way too valuable and they are not doing *nearly* enough to deserve it.

CHAPTER 4

ROYALTIES: DON'T SPEND ALL YOUR PENNIES IN ONE PLACE

Let's review where we stand so far. The preceding chapters have described some of the fundamentals of a standard record agreement. Here is the "deal of a lifetime" that the label is offering: Instead of independently paying to make your own album, the label wants you to pay to make your album *and* let the label keep the album for itself. That sounds fair, doesn't it? Besides, why would you even want to own your copyrights anyway? Mo' money mo' problems, right? Better to let the record company exploit you instead.

It is at this point that the labels would say I am only giving you one side of the argument. What an unscrupulous lawyer I am! I haven't said a thing about the *good* parts of a record deal. Sure, the company owns your masters, and the album costs are all recoupable, but in exchange for all of that the artist will get some big fat royalty checks! Every record the label sells, the artist gets a portion of the sale.

Let's Talk Turkey

It's true, when the label sells the record you just gave them, you do indeed get a piece of the money. Never mind the fact that you would get *all* of the money if you made the record yourself (and you'd get to keep the record). Let's just put that inconvenient thought aside on account of the fact that it is just too damn depressing. Instead we'll talk about what your piece of the royalties will be in a record deal. When I am advising a client on their record contract, this is usually the first thing that they want to know. So, let's talk turkey. In a standard record contract, the artist gets...

Actually, before I finish that sentence, let me first tell you a story from my second year of law school. Ah, Second Year. It was a simpler time—back when my student loan balance was a five-digit petty annoyance instead of the six-digit credit-destroying nightmare it is today. But I digress: This discussion is about your finances, not mine.

In my second year I took my first entertainment law class. I was thrilled to finally be taking a class in a legal subject that I actually cared about. I had to spend my first year taking required courses, which involved reading a bunch of boring 200-year-old cases, including one where two guys chase a fox for some reason. Apparently, that fox case is actually a very important one, although I did not pay nearly enough attention in class to be able to tell you why. I despised the required classes. However, it was worth it to get through them so that I could start taking an entertainment course in my second year.

In the third week of that class, I had my first homework assignment. Our professor emailed everyone a copy of a standard recording agreement and the sales data of a fictional artist signed to the agreement. The assignment seemed simple enough: I had to use the terms of the agreement and the sales data to calculate how much the artist should receive in royalties. It seemed that the only thing standing between me and an "A" grade on this task was to calculate the number of copies sold in the sales data and multiply it by the royalty rate in the contract. Easy peasy.

Or so I thought.

Once I got started, I quickly became frustrated as I tried to untangle the contract's labyrinthine hodgepodge of percentages, deductions, exceptions, recoupable costs, and other terms that had to be considered in reaching a final number. There were pages upon pages of clauses to examine. It became evident to me fairly quickly that solving this problem would not involve a simple act of multiplication.

I spent an entire night scribbling down and angrily erasing numbers. My dorm room floor became a graveyard of crumpled papers, each one representing yet another failed attempt to conjure an answer that made even a semblance of sense. Once I had torn through every sheet in my legal pad, I decided to move into the current century and enter the data into a computer spreadsheet to get myself organized. And, to get a better handle on how they interacted with each other, I mapped all the contract terms out on my bathroom mirror using a red dry-erase marker I had in my desk. This tactic had the unintended consequence of making it look like a crazed maniac was scrawling horrific messages in blood over my toilet. But considering what this assignment was doing to my mental state, I suppose that wasn't far from the truth (minus the blood part).

Thankfully, my new approaches finally started to bear fruit. Several hours and one ruined Friday night later, I finally came up with the answer. After checking my steps several times and recalculating the numbers to make sure, I felt confident that I had slayed the beast. I relaxed for the rest of the weekend, excited to attend class on Monday and be recognized for the entertainment law wizard that I was.

I remained assured of my calculations throughout the weekend. However, that did not stop me from engaging in one of the time-honored practices of the mediocre student: talking to the smartest kid in class before a lecture starts to make sure we had the same answer. I approached this colleague, who will likely become the youngest Supreme Court justice in American history by the time this book gets published, and compared our assignments.

My heart sank. My answer was not even close to hers. I couldn't believe it. I skimmed her logical, neatly-organized findings and realized that my hours of work were for naught. Compared to her answer, I was not even in the ballpark. I was not even in the city where they built the ballpark. I was far from being an entertainment law wizard. In fact, I was now more concerned that my analysis would constitute malpractice in most states.

The whole experience was crushing, and it was about to get worse. The professor quieted us down for class and began his lecture with a discussion of the homework assignment. And, because I am just lucky that way, he immediately called on me to share my answer with the group. Just what I needed: a public shaming to lift my spirits. I mumbled my putrid response, having to repeat it a second time after initially stuttering.

I swung my head around the room to behold a sea of confused faces. Some of them were rightfully questioning my analytical skills, while others were perhaps questioning the judgment of the Admissions Office in their acceptance of my law school application. My professor made a half-hearted attempt to spare my feelings. "That was an...interesting answer, Ryan," he said. During the brief pause that followed, the muffled giggles of my classmates filled the silence. Finally, he asked, "Did anyone else come up with something different?"

Every single hand shot up into the air, like beautiful fireworks in some kind of "Ryan is a Moron" festival. Smiling, he then called on the Supreme Court justice who eloquently volunteered her brilliant solution to the problem. His grin widened. I sank lower in my chair. As I stewed in my disgrace, he ambled over to the chalkboard in the back of the room. He grabbed some chalk and wrote down her answer and my "answer" on the board. He paused again, twirling the chalk between his thumb and forefinger as he stared at the numbers. He turned his focus back to his students. "I'm curious," he said. "Did anyone else get something different?"

Every hand shot up again.

My eyes widened. I scooted back up in my seat.

My professor proceeded to call on every student in the room, one by one. As each of my colleagues gave their answer, he wrote their responses next to the other numbers on the board. To my surprise, none of the answers were even close to being the same. It was a beautiful flurry of royalty calculation snowflakes. I studied the board, taken aback by the wide range of dollar values. Some of us had the artist making tens of thousands in royalties; others had the artist *owing* the label just as much.

The room filled with chatter. Everyone was looking at each other's calculations to see how they got their answers. It was chaos. Arguments ensued. I let out a relieved sigh, no longer worried that I was stupid. Or, if I was stupid, everyone else was too. I felt better either way. The professor waved his arms to get our attention and settle everyone down.

A student in the back shouted, "So what's the answer, Professor? Did anyone get it right?"

Our esteemed educator chortled, and then responded, "I have no idea! Your guess is as good as mine."

He taught us a very important lesson in that class. It is the same one that I impart to clients today when they ask me what their royalties will be under their record contract. Royalty provisions in a record deal are so confusing, and are open to so many different interpretations, that obtaining an accurate calculation is all but impossible. I can certainly *try* to determine what my client's royalties should be. But the truth is my client could ask the same question to ten other lawyers and get ten different responses. Record labels like the ambiguity of their contracts, because it allows them to interpret their language in a way that leaves the artist with less than they probably deserve. And, if push comes to shove, it will be extremely difficult for the artist to prove the amount by which they were shorted, should they choose to sue (assuming they can afford to do so).

This issue underscores the barrage of royalty underpayment lawsuits that major labels constantly face from big-name artists. In the last few years, superstars like Eminem, Counting Crows, and many of the American Idol contestants have been connected with litigation accusing labels of not paying enough. And the suits are only becoming more frequent as technology advances and the methods for distributing music increase. Unfortunately, there is no indication that record labels are going to improve their framework anytime soon. All we can do for now is try to sort through the contractual wreckage and try to give you *some* insight into how these royalties work. Let us begin.

Record Deal Royalty Provisions

Royalty Rate

The first number we will look at is the artist's royalty rate for each physical album sold. We will start here because this number is most prominently featured and discussed in the contract, and most of the royalty calculations are based around that number in some way. That being said, the rationale for the emphasis on physical album sales is becoming less and less valid as music technology continues to advance. As you'll see in the coming discussion, labels' preference for their prehistoric way of doing things is not a product of an inability to adapt, though they will profess that they "just haven't gotten around" to making pertinent changes. The real reason is that labels will not change their contractual relationships with artists so long as the relationship structure continues to benefit the label, but they will quickly change anything that ceases to benefit them. We'll circle back to this idea shortly.

In any event, labels' royalty provisions still primarily focus on CD album sales. This is despite the fact that consumers (1) primarily do not buy CDs anymore, (2) primarily do not buy albums anymore, and (3) are beginning to stream music rather than buy it at all. The entire market is undergoing a massive transformation, but you wouldn't know it from looking at most record deals.

Before I tell artists what their physical album royalty percentage will be under a particular contract, I often like to ask them what they *think* the number will be. The answer I hear most often is 50% of sales. Admittedly, that figure makes some intuitive sense. The artist and the label are each doing some of the work, so why wouldn't they split things down the middle? Moreover, many of the artists I work with are also songwriters who get 50-50 splits from their song publishing deals. Thus, they assume that their record contract will work the same way.

Despite providing a perfectly logical answer to my question, I am forced to inform them that the music industry is not a place for rationality. I tell them that, unfortunately, their rate is not 50%. In fact, it is much lower than 50%. Much, much lower. Many of my clients will get a CD base rate of just 15% of the wholesale price (what the store pays for the album), with some contracts even going to 10% or lower. If we assume that a big-box retailer like Wal-Mart pays $7.25 per album wholesale (a *very* generous number for an up-and-coming artist), and we use the more favorable 15% rate to calculate the royalty, this would leave the artist with about $1.09 in royalties for each CD album sold. The remaining $6.16 goes to the label.

I don't know about you, but that split seems backwards to me. Normally, the more indispensable someone is in a particular business transaction, the more money they make. This is why movie studios pay Brad Pitt a lot more money than the best boy grip. The former is much harder to replace than the latter. So ask yourself: Who is more essential to the music-making process, the artist or the label? Artists can still make music without a label (and often do so quite successfully these days). But without artists, the label is nothing. It cannot operate without someone making music for it to sell. Labels need artists to survive. And yet, they have the audacity to insist on contracts where they get six out of every seven dollars.

Recoupment

And here's the kicker: It turns out that our $1.09-per-album figure is significantly higher than the real number. There are other factors that knock that tiny figure down even further. For one thing, you can't forget about the label's best friend: Mr. Recoupment. As we discussed in Chapter 3, the artist does not get any money until the label fully recoups the album's costs (such as recording costs, independent promotion costs, the list goes on) solely from the artist's royalties. The artist gets nothing until its debt to the record label is slowly paid off, one measly sale at a time. Meanwhile, the label gets to start making its $6.16 from the moment the first record is sold.

Recoupment aside, there are yet more reasons why the artist's $1.09 is not really $1.09. The record contract has a bunch of nasty terms, which work together to push that number even lower. Some provisions lower the base price from which the royalty is calculated, while others lower the royalty rate itself in specific circumstances. I will not discuss every single one, because you are probably a good person and do not deserve to be subjected to such punishment. But I will go over a couple of the particularly painful ones.

Deductions

Some record contracts provide for what are called "Percentage of Sales Deductions." These clauses specify that the artist will only receive royalties on a certain percentage of the records sold, like 85% or 90% of sales. A "90% of sales" provision effectively knocks down a 15% royalty rate to 13.5%. And what is the label's justification for not paying you on every record it sells? So far, I have yet to hear one when I talk to executives. The rationale basically boils down to the fact that labels like money, they want more money, and they want to get more money by paying you less money. I wish they would just come right out and say that. I would appreciate their honesty, at least.

So-called "container charges" are another common deduction. Container charge provisions usually impose a 25% deduction from the price from which the artist's royalties are calculated. The label's argument for the deduction is that the some of the album's wholesale price is represented by its packaging. And since the artist did not create this packaging, they should not receive royalties for it.

There are several things that are wrong with the label's argument here. First, there is no universe in which an album's packaging is worth anywhere near 25%. Think about it: You can buy CD jewel cases in bulk for about twenty cents apiece. At that cost, the CD's "container" makes up less than 3% of the album's wholesale price of $7.25. So unless the label is melting down old platinum records to make their jewel cases, there is no way the container costs are 25%. This is just another blatant cash grab by the record company.

The second issue with this container charge nonsense is that many label contracts will try to impose this deduction in situations that plainly do not call for it. This reminds me of yet another law school story. In my first year, my school invited three major label executives to give a talk on the state of the record industry. And since every first year law student is basically either an aspiring entertainment lawyer or environmental lawyer, about half of my class turned out for the event. I had a seat in the front row, as I was eager to learn as much as I could from some experienced veterans of the record business.

Unfortunately, the only thing I "learned" that day was how much I disdained listening to experienced veterans of the record business. They spent much of their insipid two-hour presentation whining over how illegal music downloading has affected their bottom line. What they failed to mention is that labels totally exacerbated this problem by taking years to transition to online sales. They also lamented the difficulty of finding and breaking new artists, glossing over the fact that labels helped to create this difficulty by slashing their A&R, development, and promotion budgets over the last fifteen years.

After concluding their "We Brought This Doom Upon Ourselves" lecture, the panelists took questions from the audience. Standing up and grabbing the microphone, I held back the urge to ask them something snarky and overly critical. I instead asked them a softball question about how their companies have adapted their business practices to changes in technology. Their answers were expectedly long-winded and ridden with execu-speak, causing a few audible groans from the students in the crowd.

Elaborating further, one of them started talking about record agreements. "We will sort of have to wait and see how we will modify our contracts to incorporate new technologies," he said. "We still keep a lot of provisions the same, though. We even use the same container charges for digital sales. It will be interesting to see how technology will reshape our practices," he added.

My eyes widened, as if I had just heard a gunshot. I kept the mic in my hand. "Wait a minute," I barked. "Did you just say that your company charges a packaging deduction on digital record royalties? You deduct packaging for something that *has* no packaging?"

"Yes," he replied.

My jaw slowly gaped open, incredulous at what I just heard. My next words left my mouth as a sort of reflex.

"How do you people sleep at night?"

The room fell silent. My stomach immediately knotted up once I realized what came out of my mouth, but there was nothing I could have done to stop it. Several gasps began to float through the room, accompanied by some nervous chuckles. The people running the event immediately grabbed the mic from me and started taking questions from the other students.

Looking back, I was lucky that I didn't get into any trouble with my school that day. Though, to be fair, I still would like an answer to my question. How *do* they sleep at night? Seriously! Container charges are ridiculous enough when the records actually *have* containers. But many contracts will impose these same deductions on music sold through Internet downloading. While the executives' rationale seemed to be that they just hadn't gotten around to updating their contracts, there is no justification for this practice other than the one I offered before: Labels like money, they want more money, and they want more money by paying you less money. If labels are truly bound by institutional inertia of the sort necessary to legitimize such a rationale, then how is it they were able to do away with the contract provisions-of-old that provided for the labels' shouldering numerous album costs instead of passing them on to the artist? I answered this question at the beginning of this chapter. Labels have no problem changing their standard contracts as technology changes over time. But they only seem to do it when it benefits them financially.

Crunching the Numbers, or How to Make $700,000 Disappear

To get the full financial effect of the many royalty deductions that litter record contracts, you have to see what happens when all of the deductions are calculated together. Once that occurs, the numbers get really nasty for the artist. Think happy thoughts, because this is going to sting a bit:

Let's say the contract has a "90% of sales" clause. As we stated before, this means that, for basically no good reason, the label is not going to pay you a royalty on 10 percent of the records sold. This has the effect of further shrinking your already fun-sized royalty rate. Now couple that with the 25% container charge, and this means that you are no longer getting 15% of $7.25, you are getting 13.5% of $5.44. This reduces your royalty to roughly seventy-three cents on each album sold (instead of $1.09), with the label keeping the remaining $6.52.

If you ignored all the math in the previous paragraph (and who could blame you), here's the long and short of it: Once you combine those two deductions together, it means that the label is not keeping six dollars out of every seven. They are actually keeping roughly nine dollars out of every ten. And keep in mind that your measly ten percent *still* has to recover all of the recoupable costs, which has a devastating effect on your take-home pay.

My apologies in advance, because more math is coming:

Continuing the hypothetical: We will assume that your album had $60,000 in recoupable costs (which would be on the low side for a label project) and sold 100,000 copies. That many copies won't get you a gold record, but if you sold that much in this market, I'd certainly uncork some champagne for you. After all, at a $7.25 wholesale price, you and the label grossed $725,000. Not bad at all.

But remember that *you* don't see any money until your royalties cover the $60,000 in recoupable costs. At your per-album royalty figure, reduced to a meager sum of $.73 thanks to the deductions in your contract, this will not happen until the 82,192nd record is sold. You will get your royalty on every album sold after that.

After crunching the numbers, this means that you will make about $13,000 in royalties on an album that probably took you more than a year to make. Congratulations, your music career has all the lucrativeness of a minimum wage job, and you took home less than two percent of the $725,000 gross. You could have made more money waiting tables. God forbid you are in a band (instead of being a solo artist) and have to split that $13,000 four or five ways. Moreover, this figure is actually a generous estimate. It neither deducts the piece of your royalty that goes to the album's producer (reducing your rate even further), nor does it account for the additional royalty deductions buried within a record contract that I did not address in this chapter (and there are *many*).

In stark contrast to your financial misfortune, however, the record label did quite well. Unburdened by the same low royalty rate, recoupment clauses, and deduction provisions, the label took home over $700 grand in revenue to your $13,000. You have probably heard familiar stories about famous musicians who sell tons of records and still end up broke. If you have ever wondered how that happens, all you have to do is look at the math above.

What makes the above analysis additionally disheartening is the fact that the music business is not an album business anymore; it has been singles-driven for the better part of this century. Once online downloading became the primary means for consumers to obtain music, people stopped having to buy entire albums just to listen to the three songs from their favorite artists that they actually want to hear. Instead, they go online and buy the individual songs that they desire.

This change in consumer behavior means that artists make much less for each sale. Now instead of getting $.73 from each $10 retail album sale, the artist gets about seven or eight cents on each $1 single sold on a site like iTunes. Now think back to our previous example. At our new royalty of seven cents for each individual song, the artist is going to have to sell over 850,000 singles just to cover the $60,000 in recoupable costs from before. Basically, you would have to become nearly a platinum-level recording artist just to be able to break even in your record deal!

The Cross Collateralization Monster

This chapter has discussed some of the many tricks that record labels employ in their contracts to capture as much of your recording income as possible. But before we leave this discussion, let me share with you one more particularly horrid one. This contract term is the most malevolent of them all. In most cases, this particular clause ensures that many artists will make zero in royalties throughout the entire agreement. Forget even that paltry $13,000 "payday" we talked about before. This term, found in pretty much all contracts, leaves many artists with nothing—even if they are able to achieve considerable commercial success.

Here's how this destructive term works. Let's say you sign a three-album deal with a record label. You're understandably excited. The label executives have told you repeatedly that they believe in your music and they are determined to make you rich and famous—no matter how long it takes. The label releases your first album and, unfortunately, it doesn't do so well commercially. Don't feel bad. It can take years for an artist to become successful in this industry, and the label has already told you that they are in it for the long haul. That being said, you made nothing in royalties for the first album because you didn't sell enough for your cut of the revenues to recoup the album's costs. Better luck next time.

To your dismay, your second album suffers a similar fate. Despite creating great music, your work has still not resonated with the consuming public on a massive scale. Your sales on album #2 failed to recoup the album's costs as well. At this point, you've had a tough couple years. You've put your heart and soul into making two great albums, but have yet to see one dime in royalties. The record label has already made money off your albums, but you still have nothing to show for your efforts.

But then album #3 happens. Bam! You finally catch lightning in a bottle. Your music strikes a chord with the public and you achieve commercial success with your latest work. Your copies sold reach into the hundreds of thousands. Those years of toil are finally paying off. You didn't think it would take so long for your record deal to make you some money, but it looks like the label's promises of riches are finally coming true. You eagerly await the arrival of some sizable royalty checks.

35

But, to your surprise, the checks never come. You're confused. You know that album #3 had some costs to recoup, but surely your stratospheric record sales generated enough royalties to pay off the album's debts. There must be some mistake. You call a lawyer, hoping he or she will confirm your entitlement to at least some of the massive revenue your music generated. The lawyer sifts through your record contract and accounting statements, and then regretfully confirms that you are indeed not entitled to any royalties. In fact, you still *owe* the label money, and you will need to sell many more records before you are in the black.

What gives? Well, you became a victim of a "cross collateralization" clause buried within your record deal.

What does that clause mean? In a standard record contract, each album that the artist records is "cross collateralized" with the albums that follow, meaning that any un-recouped costs from one album are carried over to each subsequent album for royalty calculation purposes. Un-recouped funds for each album are not separately considered, but, rather, are all lumped together in one account balance that has to be zeroed out before the artist sees any royalties at all.

Cross collateralization is the reason why you did not make any money from your hit album in our hypothetical example. The royalties from that album not only have to recoup that album's costs, but they also have to satisfy the un-recouped balances from your previous two albums. You will likely be playing catch-up for your entire career. Your ever-swelling debt to your label will grow faster than your miniscule royalties can pay it down. And while you are struggling just to get back to zero, the label could very well make millions in revenues from your three albums.

Record contracts also use cross collateralization in other ways to put as much distance between artists and their money as possible. Many record deals will cross collateralize a current record deal with any previous deals you had with the same company. The effect is much the same as what happened in our three-album example above. Any royalties you make off your current contract will go towards satisfying any un-recouped costs from your previous contracts.

And do you write your own songs? Then the label has a special type of cross collateralization just for you! Artists who have a songwriting deal with a publisher affiliated with their label will usually have their royalties from both types of deals treated as one accounting unit. This means that you won't see any recording *or* songwriting royalties until the costs are recouped from all of your albums. So not only can a record deal ruin your future as a recording artist but, thanks to cross collateralization, it can also mess up other aspects of your entertainment career.

You Pay For the Album, You Don't Keep the Album, You Make No Money From the Album

Standard record deals are fundamentally abhorrent documents. The fact that they require the artist to bear the financial responsibility for their albums is truly awful. And it is downright sickening when you couple that with the reality that the artist does not even own the album that they paid for. But maybe labels could rationalize these downright predatory terms if artists were at least well compensated in exchange for giving up so much (In the end, I suppose everything has its price.). But, for many artists, no such fair compensation will result from their record deal.

Thanks to the harsh attributes of a record deal's royalty terms (e.g., confusing provisions, low rates, deductions, and cross collateralization), artists wind up giving up everything and getting nothing in return. What record companies do to their artists is pure exploitation, and you need to distance yourself from their practices.

CHAPTER 5
360 Provisions: The Labels' Newest Way to Reach Into Your Pocket

Requiem for a Fallen Industry

If you have any dreams of being a great success in the music industry, I have some very bad news to share with you: The music industry is dead.

You heard me. Dead. D-E-A-D. Dead! No more. Gone. The music industry is dead, its corpse was loaded into a boat, and a horde of Vikings shot flaming arrows into that boat. It pains me to be the one to tell you all of this, as I know you two were quite close. But the ol' girl is dead now. And the sooner you come to terms with all of this, the better.

How do I know the industry is dead? Because everyone says it is, that's how. What more proof do you need? Go ahead and type "The music industry is..." into Google. The first autocomplete result you're going to get is "...dead." Seriously, that's not a joke. By the way, that search term has over 337 million results. Oh yeah, the industry is super dead.

And if you want to know how it died, go ahead and click one of those 337 million pages. You will undoubtedly find articles that can shed some light on this horrible tragedy. They will tell you how the industry's decline came as a bit of a shock to everyone, especially when you consider how the industry was at its healthiest less than a decade before it met its untimely demise. In the late 1990s, the music business was at its peak. The emergence of the CD in the 1980s ushered in an era of high profit margins for record companies due to the medium's high sound quality and low production cost. After adjusting for inflation, recorded music revenue in the US more than doubled from the late 80s to the late 90s. The industry became a multi-billion dollar powerhouse with better domestic sales than either the movie or video game industry.

So how could something so strong perish so quickly? What could possibly kill this commercial colossus? Why, the same thing that killed the horse-and-buggy industry, the milkman business, and face-to-face conversation with other human beings: modern

38

technology. The rise of MP3s, which could store music using only a fraction of the drive space that a CD required, made it possible for almost anyone to download music online. The Internet quickly replaced brick-and-mortar stores as the consuming public's preferred means to obtain their favorite songs.

The effects on the industry were extremely disruptive. For one thing, Internet downloading transitioned the record business from being album-driven to being singles-driven. This new model meant that people no longer had to pay for a twelve-song album at a store just to get the singles that they actually wanted to hear. But while this change in purchasing habits certainly had a negative effect on record revenues, this alone did not kill the music business. You see, the real problem was not the new technology in itself, but rather how the industry reacted to it. Or, to phrase it more correctly, failed to react to it.

The true culprit for this death was not Internet downloading. It was the labels' glacial response to the technological changes affecting their industry. Instead of trying to find a way to profit in this new digital environment, record companies held tight to their world of CDs and brick-and-mortar stores—even as that world was quickly crumbling around them. Unwilling for several years to provide a legal means for consumers to download their products, people instead turned to illegal file sharing websites like Napster, which at its peak had over 60 million users.

Eventually, the labels got around to embracing the new paradigm and reluctantly started licensing their music to online stores like iTunes. But by then, the damage had already been done. Many of those who turned to illegal downloading in the face of the labels' resistance to change will never purchase a record legally again. Music sales declined precipitously starting in the early 2000s, causing an era of unprecedented downsizing and corporate consolidation in the record industry. By the end of the new century's first decade, recorded music revenue in the United States collapsed to less than half of its late-90s peak.

So there you have it. The music industry is dead. And it is time for you to give up on your dreams and move on to something new. After all, there is no use in trying to grow crops on barren soil. May I suggest pursuing another line of work? Almost any job would be better. Just don't go to law school. If you think music has no job opportunities, you should see the hiring statistics for lawyers.

But seriously, give up on music. There's nothing for you here. Go put this book down and enroll in a trade school or something. People always need plumbers.

Have you given up yet?

Why are you still reading? Did you not hear the statistics I just told you?

Are you even listening to me, hello?!?

Still Alive and Kicking

You're still here, huh? I figured you would be. You were probably already somewhat familiar with the current state of the music business, and that has not stopped you from pressing forward with your ambitions. The endless articles out there declaring the industry's demise will not deter you because your passion is too strong. I like that! I bet you can't imagine yourself doing anything with your life other than making music, and you will stay the course no matter how bad things are. Kudos to you. You will not be dissuaded by all of the voices out there pronouncing the death of your livelihood.

And because I admire your spirit, I would like to share some good news with you: The music industry is actually NOT dead. It turns out that all of those 337 million articles happen to be wrong, and I was lying to you earlier. Consider all of that a test of your resolve, and you passed! Ignore the conventional wisdom. To play upon the famous Mark Twain quote: Rumors of the music industry's death have been greatly exaggerated. In fact, the industry is perhaps stronger than it has ever been. And talented artists who work their tails off, exploit the right opportunities, and have enough luck can make a damn good living for themselves. I am privileged to have worked with some amazing clients who have done exactly that.

Given all of the information I have previously told you, it is reasonable for you to ask how I could possibly say the music business is thriving. How can an industry that has seen half of its record revenues vanish over the course of a decade be considered healthy? How can an industry succeed when people can steal its product with just the click of a mouse?

40

Here's how: To view the preceding information as evidence of the industry's death is ultimately narrow-minded. It's true that record sales have fallen into the cellar. And illegal file sharing is a very big problem that warrants stronger enforcement. But these problems are just affecting the *recorded* music industry, which is but one segment of the music industry as a whole.

Just because record companies, which dug their heels in rather than adapting, ruined the record business does not mean that the rest of the music business is failing. Buying music from stores is just one way people consume music, and it turns out that the other ways to consume music are doing better than ever. During the same time period when record sales were cut in half, U.S. concert ticket revenues have more than tripled. Additionally, music streaming has exploded since the close of the previous decade, currently accounting for nearly one-quarter of the industry's total revenues (and quickly rising). People might not be buying copies of music as much anymore, but they are listening on subscription-based and ad-supported streaming services in droves.

What's more, that same Internet, which seems to be eroding the record business, is providing significant lifts to other sectors of the industry. Online retailing has boosted music merchandise sales, as it is easier than ever now to provide fans with t-shirts, posters, and all sorts of other trinkets. The Internet allows even small-time musicians to sell merchandise. The presence of online storefronts like Amazon and Etsy mean that any musician can easily peddle their wares unburdened by the strictures of physical supply chains. And online print-on-demand retailers like Cafepress, Spreadshirt, and Zazzle allow musicians to create merchandise without having to make significant volume investments.

The recent growth of other sectors of the entertainment industry has also been lucrative for musicians and their works. TV programs (including commercials), films, and video games all need musicians, songwriters, producers, and engineers to make the music featured in their respective media. And all of these sectors have grown considerably in this century—particularly video games, which have seen their sales nearly triple from 2000-2010.

Our favorite movies, television shows, and games all employ music professionals to create songs for their programs. Moreover, these mediums also pay handsomely to use pre-existing songs in their products. Every time you hear a song in a TV commercial or in the latest *Grand Theft Auto* incarnation, the producer of that project paid an artist (or label) to use that song. Those sort of licensing revenues generate over $300 million each year for the music industry. And that number is poised to rise quite a bit in the coming years.

What all of this is meant to show you is that the music business is definitely not dead; it has just been transformed. More than ever, being a successful musician means more than just selling records. Those who prosper will be the ones who can make the most of the many different revenue streams available to them. The musicians that succeed will be the ones who can sell records, *and* perform killer live shows, *and* create exciting music videos for websites like YouTube, *and* develop and sell interesting merchandise, *and* effectively license their music in other media.

Breaking the Labels' Fall

So this is the world in which we live now. While every other sector of the music industry is doing just fine, the inflexible record companies ran their sector straight into the ground. Labels are hemorrhaging cash now, and they need someone to stop the bleeding. I'll give you one guess as to whose pocket they pillage to fatten up their shrinking bottom line.

You got it; it is the artists who pay for the labels' incompetence as labels try to get even more money from them. "But, how can record companies possibly squeeze any more dollars out of their artists?" you may ask. As noted in the previous chapter, nearly all of the record revenues produced under a record deal already go to the label. So it would seem that their artists have already been bled dry.

Au contraire! If there's one thing labels have always been good at, it is finding ways to siphon more and more money off of their signed talent. Record companies have noticed the success that artists are having in other areas of the music business, and they want a piece of that action. They don't want to do much of anything to actually *earn* that money, but they still want it because money is great and they like buying things. Enter the labels' latest artist-plundering innovation: the 360 provision.

360 Provisions, Generally

This provision goes by many different names in record contracts. I have seen labels call it a 360 Clause, Other Activities Income, Non-Record Income, Entertainment Rights, Revenue Sharing, and Brand Equity. "Brand Equity" is my favorite of these. It almost makes it sound like the provision is a good one for artist. After all, it has the word "equity" in it. How can it possibly be bad? Sure your record deal stinks and you haven't made any royalties off of your albums, but at least you're getting some sweet, sweet "brand equity" out of the deal, whatever *that* means.

What is a 360 Provision?

But whatever term they decide to use, these provisions all serve the same function. 360 clauses entitle a record label to a set percentage (often as high as 30%) of the money a recording artist earns in the other areas of their entertainment career (with the exception of songwriting income, usually because the label has already signed the artist to a similarly-predatory publishing deal anyway). 360 deals became all the rage in the 2000s. Today, almost every major label contract has 360 elements in it. Remember what we discussed before—record labels are as nimble as they want to be when it comes to changing contractual terms to their benefit.

What makes things worse about these deals is that they always seem to define "entertainment income" very broadly. This entitles the record label to a wide variety of your income, even income that is only tangentially related (if that!) to the selling of records. Did you make money going on tour? The label gets a cut. Did you sell hats and T-shirts with your name on them? The label gets a cut. Maybe you have some acting chops and have appeared on some TV shows. Maybe you've been in movies. Perhaps you will write a book at some point. Those are all very cool things for an entertainer to do. So congratulations for that! And congratulations to your label as well, who will get nearly one-third of every dollar that will come in for those ventures (and remember we're talking thirty percent of *revenue*, not profits).

43

The "Justifications" for 360 Deals

Apologies in advance for my lack of eloquence, but 360 deals just plain stink for the artist. It's bad enough that record contracts take nearly all of an artist's recording income, but now the labels want to get their mitts on the rest of artists' money as well. Look, their job is to sell records. In exchange for doing that, they get some (read: nearly all) of the money from the records that are sold. But in what universe should the label be entitled to a piece of things like live performance and merchandise sales? They generally will neither directly invest nor play any direct role in augmenting those revenue streams, so why should they get money from those areas?

When I make this point to record companies in contract negotiations, they unfailingly spew the same three counterarguments:

Give Us Your Money, Because Times Are Changing

The first one goes something along the lines of "Hey, the music industry has changed. Musicians don't just record music anymore. They make money in lots of different ways now, and the 360 deal helps capture that fact."

Oh, the lunacy. First of all, it takes so much effort for me to control my anger every time an industry suit pontificates to me about the "changes" happening in their industry. I am not disputing that the industry is changing. In fact, the industry changes all of the time; just as it is in life, change is perhaps the only constant in the music business. What I take issue with is that the labels only seem to give a damn about these changes when doing so is in their immediate financial interest. The industry was certainly changing back in 2000 when Internet downloading emerged, but the labels did nothing to adjust their model because CDs were still profitable for them at the time. And when downloading eventually became the standard means for consumers to buy music, did the labels change their contracts to remove container charge deductions? Of course not. Responding to that "change" would mean less money for them.

Now, the industry is changing again. But this time the change is that artists are earning a higher proportion of their income from non-record sources. Record sales are tumbling, and labels see the dollars their artists are making in their other ventures. So *now* the record companies want to trot out the "our industry is changing" argument because 360 deals mean more money for them. Unbelievable.

Give Us Your Money, Because Somehow it will be Good for You

After I endure their first piece of nonsense, the labels will unveil their second "argument" to defend these asinine clauses. In this argument, they try to claim that the label taking 30% of the artist's money is actually *good* for the artist. "The 360 deal means that we will be more invested in every aspect in the artist's career," they state proudly. "We will have an interest in growing your client as an all-around entertainer. We will have a motivation to find the artist opportunities in other media. We will be partners in the artist's success."

Partners! Yup, that's totally what my clients want—a partnership. In fact, my clients are always telling me how they want their thieving, unscrupulous, and incompetent record label to be *more* involved in their entertainment career. Definitely seems like a winning proposition for them! That being said, I will usually try to feign some willingness to entertain their argument: "I see. So what you are saying is that this is really about creating opportunities for my client and making them more successful."

"Absolutely," the label declares.

Then my usual response follows: "Okay. That being the case, then you will surely agree to limit taking your 30% cut from only the entertainment opportunities that you actually *find* for my client, instead of getting 30% of everything, which would include opportunities you had nothing to do with obtaining."

"Oh no," they reply. "We will get the 30% for everything."

"Hmm. That doesn't exactly give you much of an incentive to actually find opportunities for the artist, seeing as you will get your money either way. But, oh well. I'm *sure* you still genuinely care about my client's development," I say. Then follow up by asking, "How about this: Since you talked about investing in his career, how about providing some start-up funding to help him develop new

45

career opportunities? Maybe give him some tour support and initial capital to create some merchandise?"

"No. We're not doing that either," they answer.

"Ah. So this is really just about you making money while having to expend as little effort as possible. Got it," I finish.

More and more, you'll hear record labels talk about wanting to be more involved in all of the aspects of their artists' career, and they will suggest that the 360 deal is the best way to align the labels' interest with the artists'. But in my experience, despite the labels' lofty promises, the only thing these 360 provisions seem to get labels more involved with is the artist's wallet. Besides, the last couple decades of sales data show that record labels can't even sell records well. Why on earth would we want them playing a role in the other areas of the entertainment business?

Give Us Your Money, Because We Said So!

Once we've swatted away their pseudo-magnanimous "our 360 deal is actually good for the artist" argument, we find that the labels have one more arrow in their quiver. This time, they dispatch with any notions of trying to benefit my client and instead say that the provision stays in because the label *deserves* it. "It's like this," they say. "If it were not for our company's hard work in making your client a successful recording artist, he would never have become famous enough to get all of these other opportunities in the entertainment industry. He would never become a movie star, or a bestselling author, if it weren't for all of the records we sold for him. Consequently, we deserve to share in the artist's income in those areas."

It is certainly a puzzling argument, to say the least. First of all, it presupposes that labels are not already adequately compensated for the things they do. I'm not sure how they can claim *that* with a straight face. In exchange for the "support" that a label gives an artist in their music career, the label already gets to keep nearly all of the revenues from the artist's record sales, and the artist is obligated to pay back all of the label's financial contribution to the project through recoupment. The resulting income for the label can easily be seven figures or more with a hitmaking artist. That certainly seems like a more-than-fair deal.

And there is also something else troubling about the label's argument here. It seems to be based on the notion that, if a company provides a service for a customer, and is compensated for that service, the company should still get a percentage of the customer's overall income because that service may have indirectly increased said income. God help us if other businesses worked that way:

For example, I happen to love McDonald's breakfast sandwiches. They are so good! I am ashamed to say that I might even be a little addicted to these greasy delights. Frankly, if I try to start my day without an Egg McMuffin, there is no way I will be as productive. Now, imagine if McDonalds became aware of this fact, and said to me: "Ryan, if it weren't for our restaurant's hard work in giving you the fuel you need to be the best lawyer you can be, you would never be as good at your profession."

I can't dispute that, unfortunately.

They go on: "Our efforts helped make you a success at your job, so it is only fair that we should receive a set percentage of your paycheck each month. We expect payment starting next month. Thank you for your business."

This obviously sounds absurd, but, in this example, America's #1 fast food chain is just trying to sign me to a 360 deal, which record labels do all the time. And, if anything, McDonald's probably has a better argument than the record label has. A hearty breakfast has far more of an impact on my abilities as a lawyer than a record label has on their clients' abilities to act in movies, after all. 360 deals are not about fairly compensating record companies. Labels are already more than fairly compensated. These deals are about greed.

Moreover, if record labels insist on clinging to this "we deserve a piece of your success" argument, I think it is only fair that it should work both ways. Many superstar artists play a significant role in increasing the overall strength of their record label. The gobs of money that labels make from their most profitable artists are often used as seed money for the label's up-and-coming talent. Furthermore, labels often force their superstars to record songs with the company's fledgling artists as a way to boost the latter's profile. Therefore, if it were not for the superstar's efforts, the record label would not be as successful. So if we apply the logic that labels use for their 360 deals, then the *superstar* should be similarly entitled to a percentage of the *label's* overall earnings. Thirty percent sounds good. That seems to be the going rate, after all.

I can already hear the swift response from the other side of the table: "That's completely absurd! Our margins are razor-thin as it is. We can't afford to pay that!"

There's Just Not Enough For Everyone

Well, guess what? Neither can artists! Keep in mind that the 30% that labels demand in the 360 deal is 30% of *gross*, not net. This means that the money the record company makes from your entertainment industry activity comes off the top, before any costs are deducted.

With your label taking thirty cents of every gross dollar, one can imagine how the artist can get tapped out fairly quickly. Let's say you perform a live show and get paid. The label, 360 deal in hand, gets 30% off the top. Ouch. Next, your manager comes along. You have to pay her 15% commission (the standard rate for managers). While you loathe having to cut that check, at least the manager has done more to deserve that money than the label. She is actively involved in all aspects of your career, unlike your label, and does her work for half of the label's rate. It is a pretty good deal, all things considered. Next, you have to pay 10% to the agent who booked the show for you. And let's not forget about the 5% that goes to your lawyer who negotiated the deal and looked over your contracts.

Add it all up, and you just lost 60% of your gross revenue, with half of that 60% going to a record company that has nothing to do with putting your live shows together. With that remaining 40%, you now have to pay all of the costs of your live show (labor costs of musicians, labor costs of support staff, transportation, lighting, sound equipment, food, etc.). Oh, and there's also the little issue of taxes. That is to say, assuming you have any crumbs of income left after covering all of the above costs, you still have to pay the government its share.

After you make all of these payments, how much money do you think you will get to take home when all is said and done? Two things are for sure: (1) It certainly won't be nearly as much as the

30%-of-gross that the record company got; and (2) It would have been a hell of a lot more if you did not have to pay your do-nothing label its 360 commission.

Cross Collateralization: Revisited

Before we leave this topic entirely, I want to discuss one other aspect of 360 deals that I feel truly illuminates the labels' hypocrisy when it deals with its artists. In the previous chapter, we talked about cross collateralization clauses, which are nasty contractual provisions that have disastrous financial implications for artists. In a cross collateralization clause, all of the albums that an artist records for a record company are treated as one accounting unit, and therefore an artist does not receive any royalties from any of their record deals until all of the artist's debts from all of their albums are recouped. This clause eliminates nearly all of the financial risk for the label while leaving the artist broke in the process.

As we also examined in the previous chapter, labels often like to expand the scope of cross collateralization further than that. Some contracts have clauses that treat an artist's recording and songwriting income as one accounting unit. Thus, the artist would not receive any recording or songwriting royalties until the costs are recouped from all of their albums. Basically, labels love to cross collateralize stuff. When record executives are not eating, sleeping, or pillaging, they are most likely cross collateralizing something.

Considering that this practice is basically second nature to them, I will usually try to negotiate the following slight tweak to any 360 deal that a label wants to force down my client's throat: "Since we are treating everything else as one accounting unit," I will say to the label, "how about we also treat the 360 income the same way? How about you guys cross collateralize the 360 income the label receives against the artist's debts to the label? You can apply the 30% you are getting from my client's other entertainment industry activities to help pay down the artist's recoupable balance."

If the label were to do this, it would actually be an instance in which cross collateralization would *help* the artist. It would zero out the artist's recoupable debt faster and thus allow the artist to earn record and songwriting royalties sooner. And it seems like a fair thing to do. If the label is already going to use the artist's record royalties and songwriting royalties to pay down the debt, why not throw the 360 income in there too?

Would that be a fair and reasonable change to any 360 deal? Yes. Would it be good for the artist? Absolutely. But have I met a single label willing to do it? Hell, no. Labels do indeed love cross collateralization, but they only love it in situations where they can make themselves richer. They only want the artist's income streams to be treated as one accounting unit when doing so is in their financial interest. Record contracts are designed to allow the label to make as much money off of their artists as possible, while delaying the payment of any royalties for as long as possible. Labels ensure this reality through recoupment and cross collateralization clauses, which force artists to use their miniscule royalties to pay down an ever-accumulating debt that they can never possibly eliminate. Labels have no inclination to allow any changes to their agreements that could affect this lucrative arrangement—even though that arrangement has ruined so many artists' lives.

Getting Every Last Drop

For as long as there has been recorded music, there have been unfair record contracts. While the practice of exploiting recording artists is as old as phonographs and wax cylinders, the recent emergence of the 360 deal amplifies this exploitation to a whole new level. For decades, record labels have pillaged their artists, but they used to confine their pillaging to their artists' recording income. So while these contracts were wildly unfair, at least artists could still make a living in other areas of the entertainment business. Many artists could not make a dime off of their recorded music, but they could make up for it by touring, selling merchandise, and even acting, if those opportunities presented themselves.

Unfortunately, 360 deals change all of that. By taking a big chunk of an artist's non-record revenue, labels are gobbling up the last morsels of income artists have to support themselves. The labels want this money despite having no legitimate claim to it. Their incompetent and inflexible business practices orchestrated the downfall of their sector of the industry, and now they want to shore

50

up their fading profits by wringing every last dollar they can from musicians like you. You should not have to pay for the labels' mistakes with your livelihood, but that is exactly what you'll be doing if you sign a contract with a 360 provision.

CHAPTER 6

MARK IS STUCK

I, Entertainment Lawyer

I am going to say something that you will rarely hear come out of the mouth of an attorney: I love my job. A lot.

You won't hear many lawyers say things like that because the legal profession is not a very happy one. This is borne out by the statistics: About 70% of lawyers will tell you that they would choose another profession if they could, one out of every five lawyers suffers from alcohol or substance abuse, and, sadly, law has the highest suicide rate of any profession.

There are plenty of reasons why the law has become such a depressing place. The hours are often brutal, the projects can be as voluminous as they are monotonous, and the pressure is often extremely intense. What further complicates matters is that many clients only tend to come to you when they have a really big problem, which means you are often trying to help people who are extremely stressed and in situations prone to cause emotional instability.

Attorneys who work in large firms tend to have it particularly tough. In a big firm, your worth is determined by how many hours you bill to clients. Speaking in terms of firms' bottom lines, the quality of a lawyer's work product is not nearly as important as the quantity. For firm lawyers, it is not enough to be good at what they do; they also need to be working during every free moment they have. Firm lawyers often spend more than 100 hours in their offices each week, with additional hours put in at home. And while the salaries *can* be high (sometimes), if you convert that salary to an hourly wage, there are plenty of jobs that are more lucrative and a lot less stressful.

And, it gets worse. There is an even more distressed group of lawyers: the unemployed ones. The recent recession has led to mass lawyer layoffs, and currently tens of thousands of attorneys are struggling just to get one of those soul-crushing legal jobs that I mentioned above. This surplus of unemployed lawyers has left recent law school graduates—often with overwhelming amounts of debt—in the worst situation of all. Only about half the graduates of the class of 2012 were able to find a job in which a law degree was either required or preferred.

So, yeah, it's rough out there, which makes me incredibly thankful that the work I get to do is both professionally rewarding and personally fulfilling for me. I feel blessed that my job doesn't, well, suck. I think it helps that I don't work in a law firm sweatshop. Instead, I have the privilege of working alongside a small group of dedicated attorneys and other professionals in a relaxed environment. We are all good friends, and we enjoy putting our heads together to solve our clients' problems. Practicing entertainment law is a blast. I find it fulfilling to help musicians, being that I am a middling pseudo-musician myself. I also do significant work in education and intellectual property law—which are fun and fulfilling gigs as well. I am still kind of young by lawyer standards, but I can say with confidence that I can see myself doing this work and enjoying it for a long time.

But even the dream jobs have their bad days. My otherwise pleasant tenure in the law has had a few rough moments. Though they have been few and far between, I have had some difficult work experiences that made me wish I had a different occupation. The music business can be more than a little dirty, and sometimes I have worked with clients who have endured incredible suffering at the hands of their record labels.

When working so closely with these distressed artists, it is hard not to feel their pain. While our profession teaches us to maintain professional distance from those we represent, I find it impossible not to empathize with them. Lawyers are human beings with feelings (which may come as a surprise to some), and it can be emotionally taxing to help clients through really difficult problems. When working with people who are at their most financially, personally, and professionally vulnerable, I sometimes feel as much a therapist as I do an attorney. It can be an incredible burden to absorb their greatest fears and concerns. And while I would not suggest that my pain in any way compares to that which my clients feel, it does take its toll.

In this chapter, I'd like to share one particular story that caused the greatest heartbreak for me. This story involves a musician who signed a bad record deal and came to a colleague and me for help. Unfortunately, his situation was beyond repair and, despite our best efforts, there was little we could do for him. This client is always in my thoughts, and the abhorrent way he was treated by his record label motivated me to write this book.

I am retelling this story for several reasons. First, I want to demonstrate how the various destructive record deal clauses discussed in the previous chapters can interact with each other and cause permanent damage to an artist's career. Second, I hope that this story will shed additional light on the unethical business practices in which some labels routinely engage. As you read this story, ask yourself: Are these record labels the kind of organization with which I want to do business? Am I willing to entrust my music, my livelihood, and my future to companies who comport themselves this way? Am I better off trying to succeed on my own, even if it might seem more difficult at first, than to get mixed up with labels?

A quick note about this story: Maintaining attorney-client confidentiality is one of the most important professional responsibilities that lawyers have. Lawyers who reveal confidential information about their clients not only impose incredible harm upon the clients, but they can also lose their license to practice law in the process. Lawyers take confidentiality quite seriously. As a result, while this story is indeed based on real events from my practice, I have modified many of the details (as well as any personal information) considerably so as to protect the people involved.

Mark's Story

"Mark" was the guitarist for a four-member southern rock band based out of Pensacola, Florida called "Miles Around." In addition to playing in the band and writing most of its songs, Mark was the de facto leader of the group and also served as the band's manager. Even though Mark had no formal business experience, he made up for it with hard work and dedication. He ran the group quite capably.

Mark used every free moment he had to promote the band, book shows, and network with other musicians and entertainment industry professionals. Because of Mark's leadership and the band's undeniable talent, Miles Around built a respectable regional following in north Florida, as well as parts of Georgia and Alabama. People enjoyed the band's powerful, catchy songs as well as their impressive stage show, which sometimes featured Miles Around performing alongside five or six guest musicians to create a fuller sound. While the band was not quite profitable enough for its members to quit their day jobs, Miles Around was consistently playing two gigs every weekend, and sometimes even opened for superstar acts in large venues.

Eventually, Mark and his bandmates were able to save enough money to record a full album, which they sold to fans outside of their shows and on iTunes. While making the record was a more expensive undertaking than they expected, they were excited to have their music immortalized in a tangible form. They also enjoyed having an additional revenue stream. Sales from their new album brought in extra cash, which they added to their burgeoning live music proceeds.

The Record Deal

As Miles Around continued to become more and more popular, it was only a matter of time before Mark and his bandmates caught the attention of a record company. Sure enough, within about six months of finishing their album, the band inked a deal with a label. Mark and the gang had a huge celebration that day. From the day of their first rehearsal together in Mark's garage six years before, the band's goal was always to get "signed" so that they could become rock superstars. The guys were over the moon that they had finally reached the summit. After all, the band experienced some early success without a label's help and felt poised to grow, so they figured that a record deal would speed up the process and quickly make them famous around the country—perhaps the world!

Every band member signed the contract, although they all had some reservations about the document put in front of them. It was much longer than they expected it would be, and some of the language proved too complicated for them to understand. Despite these concerns, none of the members asked a lawyer look it over before they signed. The label told them it was a "standard" deal and all of the terms were customary for the industry. The band took the label at its word, and figured it would be pointless to pay an attorney to look at an ordinary record deal. In any event, the last thing they wanted to do was fight the label on any of the terms, lest they push away a company willing to offer them their big break.

The contract was a five-album deal. By the terms of the deal, Miles Around would produce a maximum of one album per year for the label and could not produce recordings for anyone other than the label while the contract was in effect. The contract would continue until all of the albums were recorded and released. The first album under the deal would be the one that Miles Around recorded before signing the contract. The band was required to transfer their copyrights in that album to the label, after which the label would re-release the album to the public.

The remaining four albums under the deal were to be recorded in the subsequent years of the contract. Further, the contract stated that, before recording each album, the label would advance Miles Around a "recording fund," which the band would use to cover the costs needed to make the album. Whatever the band did not use for recording costs they could keep for themselves. Recording fund payments, as well as most of the costs incurred by the label on the band's behalf, were recoupable from the group's record royalties. Before any album could be released, it had to be approved by the label as "commercially satisfactory."

The record deal also had a 360 provision. The label was entitled to receive 30% (off the top) of all of the non-record entertainment industry revenue any member of the band received. This entitled the label to a huge piece of the most lucrative part of the band's operation up to that point—their live shows. The 360 provision also extended to their merchandise sales.

The Release

With high hopes on both sides, Miles Around's first album was re-released by the label. Mark and his buddies loved the first couple months of label life. The company paid a modest sum to an independent promoter and, sure enough, a smattering of radio stations started playing the record's first single. The band saw their album sales increase slightly relative to their pre-signing days. They were particularly pleased to see sales outside of the southeast, which to them was proof positive that the label was expanding the band's reach. Mark was particularly happy when he opened Billboard Magazine and saw that the album snuck onto some of the genre-specific and regional music charts. While the album did not have enough in sales to crack the Top 200 overall chart, he was still excited to see the band's name in print somewhere.

The band was optimistic about their future and saw their steady upward trajectory as an early indicator of their imminent stardom. Even though they had yet to see a cent in royalties, they were confident that the money was coming. But the good feelings were not destined to last. Even though the music critics loved the album, sales remained stubbornly modest and the record failed to explode into the megahit that everyone hoped it would. Sadly, about nine weeks after the album's release, the label withdrew what little promotion budget it had initially afforded the project—the closest a label will come to officially announcing a project was a failure. As a result, the radio play quickly dried up and the album lost what little sales momentum it had accumulated. It was not long until the album's sales were lower than when the band was selling it themselves.

The band's talent and potential were undeniable, and the group was gaining considerable respect by many in the industry before the label pulled the plug. Unfortunately, Miles Around learned a painful truth about the way many record companies operate in today's music industry: It is not enough to slowly get better. It is not enough to steadily build toward greatness. Record labels have no interest in fostering an artist's gradual development. They want quick winners. If you don't hit a homerun in your first at bat, the label is going to move on. Miles Around was legging out a base hit, but that was not going to cut it.

Mark and his friends were understandably distraught over what was happening to them. Their tenure of being signed to a label was leaving an awful taste in their collective mouths. The record contract was supposed to be the realization of their dream, but instead they lost a year of their professional lives. Not only had their record deal failed to produce a single dollar of income for any of them, but they had lost their most valuable possession in the process. Their album, which they had completely financed and recorded themselves, now belonged to the label. Even though they were the album's creators and their musical performances were embodied on each track, they could not sell or exploit their recordings in any way without the label's permission. American copyright law may provide the band the opportunity to get their master rights back in about thirty-five years, but the album will be worthless by then and they will be too old at that point to do much with it anyway.

The Label Option

The band's decision to work with a label was turning out horribly. They had lost everything and gained nothing from their record deal but a year's worth of hard lessons. But as bad as all of this was, what they didn't know was that their nightmare had only begun.

After seeing their promotional budget cut off and their sales plummet, the band had a pretty good idea of what was coming next. As with any once-beautiful relationship that eventually turns sour, they figured it was only a matter of time before they got dumped. Since the label gave up on promoting the first album so quickly, the group assumed that the executives had lost faith in the band and that Miles Around would be dropped from the roster.

Even though Miles Around had technically signed a five-album deal, the length of the deal actually turned on whether the label would continue to exercise its contractual option to have the band record a new album. These "label option" provisions are a common attribute of record deals, and they allow labels to end the deal whenever they want. Given the failure of their first album to take off, the band was sure that the label would refuse to exercise its option for a second album. They felt like dead men walking, dreading the imminent day when the axe would fall.

After a few more weeks of being in limbo, Mark finally received a certified letter from the label. But it was not the Dear John missive he expected. Instead, it was a short note from someone in the Business Affairs department informing him that the label was "picking up its option for the second album." Mark was astonished. Their dream was not dead after all. Despite everything that happened, the label seemed to be giving them another shot. He was especially surprised that such a spectacular pronouncement came via a brief, impersonal legal document. He wondered why news like this would not have at least been accompanied by a phone call, perhaps from an enthusiastic record executive congratulating them on their continuing relationship. But he was not about to let any of that ruin his good mood. Mark took his bandmates out for drinks that night and they happily celebrated their second chance at stardom.

A short time later, a label representative contacted the band and directed them to start putting together a new album. Mark rallied his colleagues to give the project their very best effort, but he knew that motivating his friends would be a challenge. They were all eager to move their careers forward, but the last few months were emotionally taxing on everyone. They were burnt out from the stresses of the last album cycle, and a couple members in particular felt that the label left them insufficiently supported, and insufficiently compensated, throughout the entire process. They told Mark they were concerned that the label would "give up" on the second album like they did the first.

Wasn't There Supposed To Be Money?

Mark brushed the concerns aside, assuring his friends that their best days were ahead and that their record deal was bound to make them rich and famous. Miles Around started plugging away on the new album, putting in eighteen-hour days writing, rehearsing, and recording in the same Pensacola studio where they laid down their first effort. When they were able to record rough cuts of songs with which they were particularly pleased, they would send the MP3 to their label representative. Several weeks after receiving the material, the label started sending vague, terse responses back to the band indicating that it "did not hear a hit" and that the tracks "were not commercial enough."

The band's drummer adequately captured the group's frustration: "They aren't telling us what they don't like about the music. What do they want from us? What does 'not commercial enough' even mean? Screw it! Let's just record what we want. As long as the fans like the music, that's what matters."

Mark was quick to remind his colleague of the realities of their circumstances. "The label has approval rights over the album.

If they don't like the music, they won't release it. We have to make these recordings their way," he told them.

The bassist chimed in: "This whole thing stinks! And by the way, these recording costs are getting expensive, Mark. Shouldn't the label be sending us some money by now? If these guys want the album done their way, they should at least be paying for it."

His bandmate was right. The record deal required the label to send the band a recording fund to pay for each album. Mark was fully aware of this. In fact, from the start of the recording process for the second album, Mark had repeatedly contacted the label about receiving the fund. Unfortunately, he had yet to receive a response to, much less any money from, his inquiries. Instead, the band was funding the album out of their own pocket, and it was quickly making them broke.

The Lawyers

Eventually, the band's money dried up. Yet, the label continued to ignore Miles Around's request for their recording fund. Desperate to finish their album, the band contacted one of the attorneys with whom I work to see if there was anything that could be done to force the label's hand. My colleague and I teamed up and decided to give them some advice pro bono—not that they were in a position to pay us anyway.

Despite having no other options, the band still felt guilty about "getting lawyers involved." Like many artists, their heads had been filled with lies from self-interested music executives who told them that "lawyers only make things more difficult" and that "a lawyer is only going to complicate our relationship. We want to keep things simple." Rest assured, when artists are told that lawyers should not be a part of the relationship, they only mean the *artist's* lawyers. You better believe that the label has a ton of lawyers on their side—smart lawyers who are paid lots of money to draft nasty contracts that make the label rich and the artist poor.

Artists need to make sure not to listen to this nonsense. The phrase "lawyers only make things more complicated" or "let's not get lawyers involved" was spoken at some point during many now-deceased music careers. Contrary to what labels may tell artists, lawyers only "complicate" things because they can force labels to actually do their jobs and keep artists from getting royally screwed. Record deals are a bad enough idea for an artist even if the artist has a lawyer actively involved in every step of contracting process. Without a lawyer, they are a complete nightmare.

Miles Around reached out to my colleague and me very late in the process. Ideally, we would have preferred that they retained us before they started self-funding their second record (or better yet, before they signed their record deal in the first place). But we reviewed their paperwork and hoped that a solution would emerge. Our hope was that we would discover that the band was indeed entitled to its recording fund and that we could simply reach out to the label as the band's legal counsel to get our clients paid. Labels have no qualms about ignoring their artists when it is convenient for them to do so. But they tend to respond when a lawyer is doing the contacting.

"We're Completely Stuck"

We also reached out to Mark to ask him about the other aspects of the record deal. Before rendering any kind of legal advice, it is imperative for lawyers to get as full of a picture as possible. This case would be no exception.

"Tell us about the 360 provision you guys signed," we asked. "Your contract says that you are required to pay them 30% of all of your non-record revenue, such as your live performance income. Have you been making those payments?"

Mark's shoulders slumped. "Honestly, we paid them as much money as we could, but not all of it. And, it's impossible for us to keep books for the money we had coming in. We're not accountants," he told us.

"That's understandable," I replied. "You guys are still pretty early in your career, so it's not like you are going to have a sophisticated business operation yet."

"Exactly!" Mark exclaimed. He took a beat, then added, "And that's not even the biggest problem with the 360 stuff. The real issue is the percentage. It is just way too high! If we paid them 30% of the money we had coming in, we wouldn't be able to eat. We can't pay them 30% off the top, *then* pay all of our costs for our live shows, and still have enough to live on after splitting the money five ways. I know we are supposed to pay it. I know that we signed a contract. But the money just isn't there."

Mark paused for a moment, expecting a judgmental reaction from us. We didn't give him one, but he continued to defend himself, as if he thought he was talking to two people who did not agree that he should be able to keep all of what he earned. "We're barely making enough to scrape by as it is. And it's not like they are helping to promote our live shows or anything. In fact, they haven't done anything to promote our band in almost a year! What are they doing to deserve that money?" he said.

We continued to offer no rebuttal to his declarations.

"Besides," Mark's voice cracked, "we figured it was all okay because the label has never asked for their 360 share. Not once. For them to do that, they would actually have to speak to us, which they never do anymore unless they are giving us unhelpful and vague criticism about one of the tracks we are recording. We don't know what to do anymore. We're completely stuck."

I put my hand on Mark's shoulder, sensing that he was becoming increasingly distressed. "I'm sorry that your band has had to deal with these difficulties," I said. "Unfortunately, what you guys are going through is something that many fledgling artists experience when dealing with record labels. Stories like these are all too common in this industry, and it's horribly unfortunate. We will look over your file and see if there is anything we can do."

Mark thanked us for our time. And though he was able to eke out a smile as he shook our hands, his eyes betrayed a feeling of pessimism about his future. I wanted to make him feel better. I wanted to assure him that everything was going to be okay, that we would be able to solve his problem and swiftly get his band out of their mess. But I knew better. I didn't tell him right then and there— mainly because I still had to review the rest his file to be sure—but I already knew that Mark and his band were screwed. They were completely, utterly, and incontrovertibly screwed, and it was too late to help them.

A Brutal Contract

What I would eventually have to explain to Mark was that Miles Around was bound to a record contract that was perfectly designed to keep them poor while the label profited off their labors. It expertly combined the various destructive aspects of record deals in such a way as to keep the band in a state of quasi-slavery from which they could not easily escape. The contract had the effect of forcing the band to continue making album after album for the label for no compensation. Meanwhile, the label would keep every cent of record sales while taking on *zero* financial risk.

Please don't misunderstand—it isn't my intention to give the label any credit for crafting this scheme. What Miles Around fell victim to is an old ploy. Other labels have been executing similar versions of this plan for decades. Miles Around was just one of many victims, and there will be many more until artists fight back and drive the label-based model out of the music industry.

Here is how this label heist worked:

1) The label finds an up-and-coming artist that has already made its own album. Filling the band's heads with promises of mega-stardom, they sign the artist to a multi-album deal.
2) The term "multi-album deal" makes it sound like the label is committing to a long-term investment in its new group, but in reality this just means that the label can force the artist to record music for the label and nobody else for years to come. If the relationship goes sour (which it does about 105% of the time), the artist cannot get out of the deal until it makes every single album required under the contract.
3) The label will use several contractual provisions to ensure that the artist is stuck with the label for years. First, the contract will state that the artist can release a maximum of one album during a specified time period (usually on a twelve- to eighteen-month cycle). This prevents a disgruntled artist from recording multiple albums at once (such as a double album) to break free from a bad record deal faster.
4) Second, the contract affords the label discretion over the album's production and timing of release. Since none of the

artist's recordings can see the light of day without the label deeming it "commercially satisfactory" (whatever the hell that means), the label can basically keep an album in development limbo and effectively freeze the artist out of the recording business for as long as the label wishes.

Miles Around fell right into this trap. The label lost interest in the band because they did not take off right away. But rather than let the band out of their deal and risk them making it big on their own (which would be embarrassing for the label), it picked up the album option to tie them down. When the label told Mark that it was not dropping the band, he thought they were getting a second chance. What he was now discovering was that the label was just using its option provision to silence a band that it no longer wanted to make music. The label then did everything it could to prevent a new release from ever happening, including not funding the record and exploiting its creative control powers to grind the recording process to a halt. Miles Around was stuck. Their label did not want them to release their music, and if they tried to release music on their own, they would be in violation of the contract.

5) The contract employs a 360 provision, which forces the artist to pay an impossibly high percentage of their non-record revenue to the label. Moreover, the label is not required to provide any support for the artist's non-record activities; so it gets the money for nothing.

6) Most up-and-coming artists cannot afford to make the 360 payments and still cover their expenses. They pay as much as they can, but fall well short of the required thirty percent. After all, the money is simply not there. The artist is understandably worried. But, much to the artist's surprise, months go by and the record label does not ask for any payments. The artist thinks that the label is giving them a break. The artist will eventually find out that this is not the case.

7) What the artist does not know is that the label doesn't care about the piddling amounts of 360 payments they are owed unless and until the artist's career takes off and bigger dollars

are in play. The label won't say anything about the money they are owed in the meantime—preferring instead to allow the artist to miss payments. This gives the label leverage in case the artist decides to try to enforce one of their rights under the contract at some point in the future (see Step 13, below).

8) At some point, the label releases the band's first album. Under the contract, the band transfers the copyright in the record to the label. However, since the band made the album before the contract began, the label does not have to pay for any of the recording costs—and even if it did, those costs would have been recoupable anyway. As a result, the label gets an album to sell (and own) without spending a dime of its own money.

9) The label will usually make a nominal effort to promote the album, but it will cut off the promotion budget (much of which is also recoupable) and move on to another project if it isn't an instant hit.

10) If the album is a hit, the label keeps nearly all of the record's revenue despite investing almost nothing in the project. If the artist is lucky, he might get a few shekels in royalties. If the album is not a big hit, the label will still make some money, but the artist won't see a single check (the artist has to repay that promotion budget, remember?).

11) Even if the album is not a big hit, and the label no longer believes in the artist, it will usually exercise its right under the contract for another album anyway. Why would it do this? If the label has lost faith, why try for a second album? Why not just let the artist go? This action is especially puzzling if you assume that the label will pay the artist a recording fund for the next album, as it is seemingly obligated to under the contract (unlike the first album, which it got for free).

12) Rest assured, the label has no intention of paying for the second album, either. Instead, it will simply let their once-beloved artist languish in a sort of contractual purgatory in which little to no music will get made. It might gently ask the artist when the record will be done, but it will not aggressively push for its completion. The label would

65

actually be perfectly content with the artist not producing anything and staying out of the industry completely. However, if the artist wants to make the record, and struggles forward against the odds, he or she will soon find that the label won't cough up a dime to help them do it.

13) How can the label get away with this? That's easy. If the artist complains about not receiving their recording fund, the label simply ignores the artist. Why not? The label has no fear of being sued by the artist, since it knows damn well that the artist can't afford to pay a lawyer to litigate. Moreover, even if the artist was able to sue to try to collect the unpaid fund, the label will respond by countersuing to collect any 360 payments it is owed.

14) The artist winds up in a rather nasty rock-and-a-hard-place scenario. If they want to make more music, they have to pay their own costs. Eventually, and rather quickly, the artist will run out of money because the label is gobbling up nearly all of the revenue from the artist's record sales. And without any other available means by which to create and release their records, the artist's career in the music industry will die.

15) Meanwhile, things could not be better for the label. It did not have to finance the artist's first record, nor will it have to finance any of her subsequent records despite the requirements of the record deal. But they will always be able to profit from any music that the artist does manage to create.

Sadly, Miles Around became a victim of this nasty scheme, which is indicative of the sort of unethical business practices in which labels often engage. By using several destructive provisions common to record deals, the label owned and will continue to own every record the band will make for the foreseeable future—and will never have to pay for any of the records! It is the very definition of exploitation.

A Bad Outcome for the Artist (and the Consumer)

Discovering what this record label had done to this promising young band left a sickness in my stomach that may never fully abate. Realizing that there was little, if anything, I could do to help them was my darkest moment as a lawyer. The label designed a scenario in which Miles Around was left with two choices: give the label records for nothing, or be finished in the music business.

Mark and his bandmates were not the only victims here either. Their fans, which were growing in number, would be permanently deprived of the band's music simply because some corporation no longer deemed it cost-effective to release the product. All of us, whether musician or consumer, should find it very troubling that a record label can silence the music of artists who are not sufficiently profitable for the label—regardless of how badly some fans might want to hear the artists' new songs. Mark and his friends remained pinned under the weight of their predatory record deal. Their contract broke them, and it is quite unlikely that they will ever make another piece of music again.

Blame the Band?

When I have told this story to others, I inevitably encounter a small handful of people who feel no sympathy for the band. "No one forced them to sign the contract," they will retort. "Maybe next time those idiots will read something before they commit to it!" is another common refrain. The band's actions regarding the 360 provision will usually face a bit of criticism, as well: "None of this would have happened if they had just paid the label the 360 payments it was owed. That's what they get for keeping something that does not belong to them."

I can understand how one might reach that opinion (though it is not an opinion that I share). Some people love launching into a rousing "you should have done X" or "that what's you get for doing Y" personal responsibility diatribe. For those who read the above story and hold a similar point of view, I ask that you make an effort to afford some compassion to a group of people who found themselves in a bad situation. After all, we've all agreed to contracts without reading them carefully. Think about all of the online "Terms of Services" agreements you have clicked in your life without so much as a glance at the text. Resist the urge to throw stones here. All of us have done have done something like this before.

Besides, it is unlikely that reading the contract would have done them much good anyway. What makes record deals so effective as an instrument for exploitation is that the exploitative elements are well hidden. The more horrid parts of a record deal are buried deep within pages of innocuous text. And it is not like even the closest read would have revealed some kind of smoking gun "We will exploit you" clause. As stated earlier, it was actually the way that several provisions in the contract (such as the master ownership clause, 360 clause, royalty rates, label creative control, and label options) combined together to place Miles Around in a state of indentured servitude to its label.

And while it certainly would have been better for the band to make its 360 payments, it cannot be emphasized enough that the money was simply not there. A struggling band cannot afford to give up thirty percent of its entertainment revenue off the top and still make ends meet. One should also keep in mind that making said payments would have been a much easier task for the band had their label not done everything in its power to pay the band as little as possible. Also, recall that the label coldly moved on to their next project, and no longer saw fit to expend any effort to help its artists become financially secure, when the band was not an immediate smash hit.

So, for those who adopt a "blame the band" response to this unfortunate tale, try to open your mind to the possibility that this might have been a case of a group of naïve musicians who found themselves in a bind. These guys simply wanted to make a living doing what they love, and now instead they may never be able to make any music again.

But even if you think Mark and his friends were completely at fault, and the label bore no responsibility for this tragic outcome, hopefully we can all still agree with a greater point: This was a bad contract, and the music industry would be better off if record deals and record labels like this no longer existed.

Let's have a conversation on how to make that happen.

PART II

MOVING BEYOND THE RECORD LABEL MODEL

CHAPTER 7
A BETTER WAY FOR THE ARTIST

Breaking Barriers

What makes the misfortune that befell Mark, and the thousands of other "Marks" out there, particularly tragic is the sheer magnitude of the damage that record labels cause. Their practices hurt all of us—musicians and consumers alike.

In the decades that the label-based model has dominated the industry, these organizations have taken on the role of a stifling gatekeeper. The vast majority of music that we hear has to pass through a label's prism first. In a more perfect world, there would be no barrier between creators and consumers. We would be able to enjoy all of the music we want to hear and that artists want to produce—not just the music that a collection of faceless executives deemed profitable enough to give us. A better reality would be one in which the fans of Miles Around would be able to enjoy new material from the band as fast as they can produce and release it, and not have the fans' enjoyment delayed by record company politics and corporate balance sheets.

My Client's Mistake

In the course of representing him in his dealings with his label, Mark frequently asked me where he went wrong and what he could have done differently to avert his band's downfall. One answer I gave him is a piece of advice that I frequently impart to musicians: It is always best to get a lawyer involved in the artist-label relationship as early as possible. Instead of waiting until things go wrong with a label before seeking legal representation, musicians are better off having a lawyer involved from day one, reviewing the label's contract before it is signed. Even if the lawyer is unable to negotiate away the contract's more horrid terms, he or she can, at the very least, properly advise and inform the artist of its dangers.

If given the chance to review Miles Around's record deal at the beginning, I could have told Mark that he was giving up a lot of power to the label and that signing the deal would be an incredible risk. I could have told him that he would not be able to meet his

71

obligations under the 360 provision and also afford to eat. And if he chose to sign anyway, I would advise him to save every dollar he possibly could to make every single one of those brutally high 360 payments owed to the label. By not paying the label its 360 share, Miles Around gave the label all of the leverage it needed to keep them under its complete control.

I am fully aware that this advice is a tad unhelpful for my client. I know that a struggling artist cannot just make that sort of money magically appear. All the saving in the world would not have enabled Miles Around to meet its 360 obligations. Unfortunately, once my client has decided to sign his life away, "try to save the best you can" is the best possible advice I can give.

Besides, where Miles Around *truly* went wrong was not in failing to comply with the record deal, it was in signing the record deal in the first place. When the record company first approached Miles Around, it was during a time when the band was on an upward trajectory and poised for success. They had already achieved so much without a label behind them, and there was no reason why they could not continue to rise on their own.

Had the band not signed with the label, their story may very well have had a different ending. The tale of Miles Around could have been one of talented young musicians who took full control of their destiny and had no barriers between their music and those who wanted to hear it. Mark and his friends could have been not just musicians, but also entrepreneurs who ran a business empire and kept a significant chunk of their profits in the process.

Allow me to tell you Mark's story again, but this time we will entertain the hypothetical of what could have happened if the band did not sign the record deal. Let's see what Miles Around could have done with more control over their career. The story will start the same way, but will feature a much different middle and ending.

Mark's Story (Revisited)

"Mark" was the guitarist for a four-member southern rock band based out of Pensacola, Florida called "Miles Around." In addition to playing in the band and writing most of its songs, Mark was the de facto leader of the group and also served as the band's manager. Even though Mark had no formal business experience, he made up for it with hard work and dedication. He ran group quite capably.

Mark used every free moment he had to promote the band, book shows, and network with other musicians and entertainment industry professionals. Because of Mark's leadership and the band's undeniable talent, Miles Around built a respectable regional following in north Florida, as well as parts of Georgia and Alabama. People enjoyed the band's powerful, catchy songs as well as their impressive stage show, which sometimes featured Miles Around performing alongside five or six guest musicians to create a fuller sound. While the band was not quite profitable enough for its members to quit their day jobs, Miles Around was consistently playing two gigs every weekend, and sometimes even opened for superstar acts in large venues.

Eventually, Mark and his bandmates were able to save enough money to record a full album, which they sold to fans outside of their shows and on iTunes. While making the record was a more expensive undertaking than they expected, they were excited to have their music immortalized in a tangible form. They also enjoyed having an additional revenue stream. Sales from their new album brought in extra cash, which they added to their burgeoning live music proceeds.

The Record Deal

As Miles Around continued to become more popular and accumulate more fans, it was only a matter of time before Mark and his bandmates caught the attention of a record company. Sure enough, within about six months of finishing their album, a label reached out to the band and offered them a contract.

Mark and the gang were quite flattered to receive some label attention. They figured that if a record company was knocking on their door, they must be doing something right. A couple of Mark's bandmates were eager to sign the deal right away, but others in the group were not so sure. The latter set knew other musicians who had signed record deals but whose careers had yet to take off. They had also read some articles on the Internet which outlined the pitfalls of working with record companies.

Mark was on the fence. On one hand, nearly all of the veteran rock bands he grew up idolizing had signed with a label at some point. But on the other hand, he was also considering the possibility that today's bands might have access to modern technology that could allow Miles Around to achieve success without a label. Moreover, he had heard some horror stories from other musicians who signed with record companies. This left him unsure about moving forward with one. Moreover, after reading over the label's confusing contract, he was concerned about signing his name to a document he could barely understand. To help unpack the contract, he brought in a lawyer who was a friend of his.

Thanks, But No Thanks

Mark called a band meeting and had the lawyer explain the contract to everyone. After his presentation, all of the band members expressed a number of concerns to their newly-acquired counsel:

"Why should they get to own the album that we already made?"

"So our royalties pay for each new album, but the label still gets to own the albums. That's messed up."

"They're getting 30% of our live performance money? Our merchandise? How are we gonna eat?!?"

Once the lawyer further explained that, on top of everything else, the label can also keep the band trapped in the deal for years and prevent the band from releasing any new music, the entire group started feeling pretty sour about label life. After some more deliberation, the band decided unanimously to turn down the record deal and continue doing things on their own.

Baby Steps

That isn't to say that the label's offer did not benefit the band in other ways. Receiving interest from a record company was a big motivator for the group. They were more convinced than ever that they could become big-time musicians. They decided to redouble their efforts to build the band and get more fans.

They started small at first. Miles Around did not have a particularly strong social networking presence, and so the band set

74

out to fix that. They had a Facebook fan page, but they only posted on it occasionally to let people know about upcoming live shows. They began to have different band members post something new each day, giving their fans a steady stream of new photos, videos, and other content to enjoy. The band also started making their music available, and selling merchandise, on the page. To get more fans for their page, they encouraged current fans to "recommend" the group to their friends. Mark went through email addresses from past show mailing lists to find additional Facebook fans.

The band also created additional social media accounts on Twitter, Instagram, Last.fm, LinkedIn, and other sites to expand their reach. They also revamped their milesaroundmusic.com website, making it a more engaging place for people to learn about the group. They posted relentlessly on all of their online platforms and gave people as many avenues as possible to discover the band and purchase their music and merchandise. The band also created a channel on YouTube and posted new video content regularly. The YouTube channel featured clips of Miles Around performing live, as one might expect, but it had other types of videos as well. Mark hosted a "vlog" on the channel in which he talked about his life and gave updates on the band's progress. He also posted short videos of the band having drinks together, playing poker and football, and writing and recording new songs.

Their fans relished having so much access to the band they loved. People interacted with Miles Around regularly on all of the platforms, and the band members were sure to interact right back to make each fan feel special. Over the next few months, the band's popularity increased steadily. Mark was beginning to truly appreciate what the explosion of social media meant for independent musicians. Bands that knew how to make the most of websites like Facebook, Twitter, and YouTube could enjoy the sort of worldwide promotion that would have cost hundreds of thousands of dollars just a decade or two ago.

Picking Up Momentum

More promotion meant more fans, which meant more gigs. The band played everywhere they could, even traveling throughout the southeast region and beyond on long weekends to play shows that would extend their reach. They were able to promote the band more with each gig, and sell more music and merchandise. Even though Miles Around was nowhere near earning "quit your day job" money, the band was encouraged by the steady stream of dollars coming in. But rather than divide up those earnings, Mark convinced his colleagues to re-invest every dollar back into the group.

As the band's operation became more complex, it became more important to have a good business structure to keep a handle on things. The band formed an LLC and ran all of its entertainment activities through that business entity. Not only did the LLC model make it easier for the band to write off its expenses and reduce its taxes, but it also limited everyone's legal liability in the event that Miles Around was sued or went bankrupt.

Miles Around was a talented band and created some awesome music as a result. But it was only a matter of time before their fans grew tired of the first album's material and started clamoring for new content. Paying to make a new record would require liquidating the LLC's bank account, and so the band decided to "crowdfund" their next album instead. At first, Mark felt weird about "hitting his fans up" for money, but he would soon discover that his fans actually appreciated the opportunity to support the band. Their fans particularly enjoyed receiving the special prizes the band gave to those who pledged support.

With two albums worth of recorded material, a strong promotional infrastructure, a growing merchandising operation, and a busy live performance schedule, Miles Around was on the rise. Their success was not happening overnight, however. To the contrary, it was a slow ascent, and there were certainly some setbacks along the way. The band's original drummer abruptly quit to pursue a job opportunity in California. The band's van was stolen after a show in Chicago (with all of their equipment inside). The theft was so crushing that Miles Around almost broke up that same night. But with each hardship, Mark kept everyone's spirits up. Both the drummer and the van were eventually replaced, and Miles Around remained focused on their goals.

A Complex Operation

Things were getting busier. Even though Mark was an effective and dedicated manager, he was quickly realizing that he had neither the time nor the expertise to operate the group himself while still playing guitar. He needed help. Luckily, Mark's bassist had a cousin who was an accountant. They brought her in to keep track of the band's increasingly-complicated finances. In addition, Mark called upon his lawyer friend once again to handle the band's legal affairs on a more consistent basis. The lawyer was a godsend for the band. He maintained the LLC's corporate documents, reviewed all of the contracts, and even maintained the registrations for all of Miles Around's copyrights in their songs and sound recordings. The band became a sleek and efficient business entity, ready and able to support additional growth.

And grow they did. Three years after turning down their label deal, Miles Around had achieved a national reach. They were full-time musicians now, living comfortably on their entertainment income. They would not have achieved what they did without hard work, but hard work was only part of their formula for success. The band had cultivated an effective business operation to take advantage of the various opportunities that came their way.

Establishing and exploiting multiple revenue streams was a huge factor in their success. They continued to make money selling their albums, even working with an independent distributor and promoter to help move units. But selling physical and digital copies of their music was just one of the many ways they made their living. The band set themselves up with a publishing team who helped get their songs in movies, TV shows, video games, and other media. Since the band owned all of their songs and sound recordings, they would be able to profit from the royalties those properties generated for the rest of their lives (and for many years thereafter). The band's lawyer, who they now made their full-time manager as well, set them up with performance rights organizations like ASCAP and SoundExchange to make sure that they received all of the radio and Internet royalties to which they were entitled. The band's booking agent had them performing all over the country in decent-sized venues. They used footage from their live shows to create DVDs to sell to their fans. The DVDs were a nice addition to their already numerous merchandise offerings, which included hats, posters, songbooks, and the beginnings of a clothing line. Mark even started acting in independent films and writing novels, both of which were passions of his.

True Industry Success

Were they superstars? By no means. Miles Around did not have any #1 hits, platinum records, or Grammy awards to their name. But was the band more successful than many chart-topping artists? Absolutely. Since Miles Around ran their own business and did not have a record label siphoning their profits, they were enjoying much larger slices of the pie than they would have as a "signed" band. Every time Mark looked over his accountant's monthly statements and saw the significant earnings coming in from all of the band's different revenue streams, he thanked his lucky stars that they did not sign that 360 deal three years ago.

Being free from record label control had other benefits as well. Miles Around had the luxury of pursuing success on its own terms. If the band wanted to make a double album, record songs with other artists, or experiment with different genres of music, they did not have to get a record company's approval. If one of the band members wanted to make some solo music away from the group, there was no record executive lurking around the corner to squash the project. If the band did not like the way a particular song was being promoted, they had the power to change things or even fire the promoter. If they were signed to a label, they would be stuck with the promotion (or lack thereof) that they got.

They were truly the captains of their ship. And for them, the freedom to be the musicians they wanted to be was even more valuable than all of the dollars in their steadily-increasing bank accounts. Mark and his bandmates were not sure exactly what the future held, but they were happy that it was actually theirs to decide. Maybe they would become the biggest rock band in the world and perform together for the next forty years. Or maybe they would go their separate ways someday to pursue other endeavors. Either way, it was all in their control. And their hard work, creativity, and entrepreneurial spirit assured that whatever ending their story had was likely to be a happy one.

CHAPTER 8

THE OBSOLETE LABEL

The Sharks and the Hurricane

Key West, Florida is one of my favorite places to visit in the entire world. Gracing the southernmost tip of the Florida Keys, Key West is just a scenic three-hour drive from my hometown of Miami. You will be hard-pressed to find a richer combination of food, music, culture, and history in any other eight square mile area. I usually try to get down to Key West at least once a year. Every time I go there, I make it a point to go to Mallory Square in Old Town to watch the Sunset Celebration. Since Miami is on Florida's southeast coast, I never get to watch the sun set over the water where I live. But a quick trip to this beloved island affords me that magnificent experience.

Old Town has plenty of fun things to do to while you await the splendid sunset. One thing that is always on my list is stopping by the Key West Aquarium. It's not the most impressive aquarium you will ever see, but it is not without its old-fashioned charm. Its unique architecture and diverse array of sea life (despite its modest size) make it a favorite among tourists. Plus, it is adjacent to the best sunset vantage point on the island.

The Aquarium has quite a few sharks. They swim in small outdoor tanks that are separated from the open ocean by a small barrier. The sharks are fed four times a day by Aquarium staff and the feedings are open to the public. On a recent trip down to Key West, I visited the Aquarium with my girlfriend and we watched one of the feedings. While throwing fish into the maws of the excited predators below, the staff member told our tour group an interesting story about when Hurricane Wilma hit Key West in 2005. Wilma devastated the city. Its 120 mph winds tore through the island and obliterated much of Old Town. Over half of the area's homes were flooded by the resulting storm surges.

The Aquarium suffered considerable damage as well, including the fact that the rising water breached the shark tank barrier, enabling its aquatic inhabitants to escape to the ocean. But surprisingly, the staff member recounted to us, only a few sharks actually left after the storm. The vast majority of them stayed put despite having an opportunity for freedom.

After our Aquarium visit, my girlfriend and I went out to the pier to take in the sunset. After providing the standard "oohs" and "aahs" that should accompany such a moment, we started talking about the sharks and the staff member's story. I asked my girlfriend why she thought most of the sharks chose not to escape that day in 2005. I was stumped, but she is a lot smarter than me and I figured she would have a good theory.

And, indeed, she did. After a pause, she opined: "Fear of the unknown. They didn't know what was out there, but they knew that they would always have fish if they stayed."

My eyes widened. We turned back towards the sunset.

How Will You Get Your Fish?

Whenever I hear artists tell me that their goal is to "get signed to a record deal," I can't help but think about those sharks. For decades, record labels have controlled the delivery of the vast majority of the music all consumers hear, which means that they also controlled the actions and livelihoods of most recording artists. If a musician wanted to have any kind of career success, they had to submit themselves to a label. Most fledgling artists didn't have the money, expertise, or infrastructure to launch their careers without one. In effect, they were the sharks at the Aquarium. They were stuck in a proverbial fish tank and wholly dependent on a greater entity for their "food."

But then a significant event changed the dynamic, for the sharks and musicians alike. For the former group, a massive hurricane swept through, flooding their tank and giving them the opportunity to swim free and find their own fish in open water. The latter group has experienced a similar "hurricane" as well. It came in the form of the Internet and the digital revolution, which has leveled the playing field and made it more possible than ever for artists to succeed on their own.

It has never been easier or cheaper for artists to create, promote, and distribute their own music, and yet I still have artists tell me that their main career goal is to secure a contract with a record company. The open ocean is within their reach, but many still want to stay in the tank. Why? It is the fear of the unknown, coupled with the comforting certainty of label captivity. The generations of musicians that came before them did it with record companies. Most of today's chart toppers have a label behind them. And though we are seeing a recent emergence of superstar indie musicians, it is not yet a large enough contingent to convince many artists that they can swim out to sea with confidence. They are not sure if they can get the fish on their own, so they remain in the aquarium where they can feel more certain that the feedings will happen.

But here's the difference between the sharks and you as a musician. In your world, the Internet "hurricane" that is giving you a chance at freedom has also wrecked the record label aquarium quite irreparably. The storm came through and the labels utterly failed to prepare for it. People started obtaining their music over the Internet and the labels were too slow to adapt. Now they are in dire straits. The money isn't coming in anything like the way it used to, and they can't feed you four times a day anymore. In fact, you're not getting any fish at all.

The labels have seen their sales collapse in the new millennium, and they have responded by slashing promotion budgets, ceasing their artist development activity, and siphoning more money off of their musicians in the form of parasitic 360 deals. And because of the array of recoupment clauses, cross collateralization provisions, and royalty base deductions that infect the standard record deal, many label artists will never see one cent from their record sales.

Suddenly, the ocean water is starting to look pretty good.

Doing it Without a Label

If you are still not convinced that you can do it on your own, I invite you to look at this phenomenon from a different angle. I submit to you that the principal functions of labels have become obsolete in the new music industry. Everything they do, artists can now do independently.

Let's do an exercise. Ask yourself: "What do record companies do for artists, exactly?" If you feel so inclined, take out a sheet of paper and actually write down the specific things you would expect a label to do for you as an a recording artist.

Done?

Whatever. I know you didn't actually write anything. I know that you have little patience to suffer through my patronizing homework assignment. I'll just move on.

How about I give you my list? Basically, you can boil a label's services for artists down to three basic things: Recording, Distribution, and Promotion. Admittedly, one could consider my list a gross oversimplification of the services record companies provide for artists, but I think it captures the central value proposition that artists hope labels will provide for them. When you sign a record deal, you expect the company to play a role in getting your music recorded, distributed to the public in various forms and media, and promoted to consumers.

For the two of you out there who actually made a list, it is possible you might have some other items on there. Perhaps you wrote "Development," in that you would want the label to help foster your progression as an artist and help cultivate your career. That is certainly an understandable thing to expect from these companies. For the dump trucks full of money labels are potentially getting from your material, it only seems fair that they expend some resources actually fostering your growth as a performer.

Unfortunately, we are long past the era in which labels actually invested in developing musicians. After Napster ravaged the record companies' business model, labels generally lack the resources or the inclination to take on long-term development projects. If you expect to get a label's attention at all these days, you need to already have an established music product and fan base. Record companies want turnkey properties, not fixer-uppers.

You might have also written "Marketing" on your list. This is by no means a bad answer, as record companies definitely do marketing for artists (or at least they should). However, "marketing" is actually a very broad term, which refers to how an organization manages and coordinates its product, pricing, placing (which includes distribution), and promotion to conduct its business. Successfully implementing these "Four Ps" of marketing is critical for any label product to succeed, and my three label activities of

Recording, Distribution, and Promotion are all affected by the company's marketing campaign.

So now let's look back at our three principal record label services in greater detail. The following will serve to demonstrate how, in the modern music industry, artists can perform these functions independently, thus rendering record companies obsolete.

Recording

So you're an incredible music talent, you say? You have amazing pipes. Your guitar playing cures most diseases. You write songs that can end world wars and stop earthquakes. With some hard work, are your amazing skills enough for you to succeed in this business on your own?

"Not a chance," says the record label. What good is all of your disease-curing, war-ceasing, earthquake-quelling musical talent if no one actually hears your stuff? If you want to be heard around the world, you'll need recordings. And good recordings don't come cheap. Not by a long shot. Studio time for an album will set you back tens of thousands of dollars. And that does not even include the costs for mixing and mastering. Don't forget to tack on the labor costs, too. You'll need session musicians. You'll need an engineer to navigate the expensively complicated recording equipment and mixing boards in the space-age studio you'll be using. You'll also need a producer to polish your record into a platinum-selling hit. Basically, you're looking at up to a hundred grand (and possibly more) to make your little masterpiece.

Do you have that kind of scratch on you? Of course not. But don't worry; a record label has got your back! Just sign on the dotted line and the label will front all of the costs to get your oeuvres recorded. The only (small) catch is that the label will take nearly all of the proceeds from the sales of your music. That sounds kind of lame, granted, but that's the only catch. Okay, maybe not the only catch. There's actually a little more. You also have to agree that what little money the label will pay you in royalties will be used to pay back the label for funding your album. Also, the label owns the copyrights to your recordings in their entirety. Basically, it's like financing a purchase with a loan—only you don't own anything in the

83

end. So it's not completely like a loan, per se. It's more like a transaction that really, really sucks.

But if you don't like it, tough! Because this is the way things are here in 1996! You heard me: It is 1996, recording equipment is stupidly expensive, and this is the only way for you to make high-quality music. So either sign the crappy contract or go work retail somewhere! I think Tower Records or Blockbuster Music might be hiring. And much like those two marvelous companies, high-cost recording will always be a part of the music industry...

Go ahead and breathe that sigh of relief now. You most certainly are not living in 1996. *Independence Day* isn't the #1 movie in America, toy store shelves are not inhabited by red tickle-craving Sesame Street characters, and music recording is no longer the province of the uber-rich. Since that time, the emergence of cost-saving digital technologies leveled things out considerably. Quality music creation is now within everyone's reach, and record labels have lost much of their leverage in the process.

In a 2007 article for *Wired* Magazine, music legend David Byrne contended that "[r]ecording costs have declined to almost zero [in the modern music industry]. Artists used to need the labels to bankroll their recordings . . . . Now an album can be made on the same laptop you use to check email." Granted, Byrne is overstating it a bit. Modern technology has not made recording a costless activity quite yet. And a PC is certainly not the only hardware you will need. That being said, the current reality is much closer to Byrne's words than it is to the way things used to be.

With a little cash, and some hard work on your part, you can have the equipment and skill you need to make music without selling your soul to a label. Innovations in recording technology allow today's musicians to build an effective studio right in their home.

For starters, a decent home recording setup should include:
- A good computer,
- at least one quality microphone with a pop filter (don't skimp here; good microphones are *critical*),
- a set of headphones,
- an analog-to-digital recording interface,

84

- a digital keyboard,
- monitor speakers, and
- a set of XLR and TS cables to connect everything together.

If you shop around, all of those things will set you back anywhere from $500 to $1,000 (not counting the cost of a computer, which I assume you already own). Is that "almost zero," as David Byrne put it? Not quite. It's not like you have that much money lying between your couch cushions. That being said, it is not cost-prohibitive. If you can save about $50 a month for a year, you can afford to make your own high-quality music. You simply couldn't do that a couple decades ago.

The only other thing you will need is some Digital Audio Workstation (DAW) software to use your fancy new equipment, add extra sounds, and mix your recordings. The advances in DAW technology in recent years are really what has made quality home recording possible. Top-of-the-line mixing equipment used to cost a fortune and occupy several desks' worth of consoles. Today, those same functions can be done with free software that can be run on a computer, tablet, or even a smartphone.

Chances are the analog-to-digital interface you bought will come with DAW software. But if not, you can download a program like Audacity for free. If you own a Mac computer, GarageBand is also a great free (and user-friendly) program. If you want something with a little more oomph, professional DAWs like Pro Tools and Sonar are great as well, though a little pricier.

"But Ryan," you say. "I'm just a musician. I'm not an audio engineer. I can't even begin to know how to use any of this software!" Well, you can learn. You weren't a musician until you learned how to sing or play the guitar, piano, ukulele, euphonium, or whatever it is that you learned how to make sound good. But you worked at your craft and you learned how to do those things. You can learn how to use a DAW, too. Watch some instructional videos on YouTube. Find some free courses online. Beg a friend to teach you. Buy some books on the subject. Do whatever you need to do. You *can* figure this stuff out. You do not need a label to record your music. It is not worth it to give your livelihood to a record company just because you are reluctant to learn a new skill.

Some of you reading this section might be thinking that I am painting too rosy a picture: "Surely Ryan isn't saying that the recording quality of a thousand-dollar home setup is the same as a million-dollar professional studio, right?" No, they are not the same. The latter is still better overall, obviously. But the gap is getting smaller every year. And dollar-for-dollar, the home setup beats the studio palace any day.

A home studio will not give you exactly the same quality as a professional one, but the quality will still be quite good, and it will be more than what you need to start out as an independent musician. Trust me; it will get the job done. And as your career moves forward and your operation becomes more sophisticated, you will have the means to enhance your home setup with additional toys and better software.

In fact, once you start to get some money coming in, you can even rent out a more-established studio in your hometown to do some recording. You can get studio time for a very good price in some places these days now that high-quality professional studios are cheaper than ever to build. Some studios will even throw in the engineer for free if you ask them. You might even get some free studio time if you are willing to play on the projects of people who have their own studios. You would be surprised how much free stuff you can get in the music business when you are willing to do favors for other musicians.

What all of this is meant to show you is that recent advancements in technology have changed the recording game forever. Artists are no longer dependent on labels to make their music. They can make music on their own, and it will sound amazing with the right equipment and enough practice.

Distribution

Admittedly, artists who can make their own records have only solved one piece of the puzzle. They still have to be able to get that music to their fans' ears. In the past, distributing music was an expensive and complicated process. For that reason, artists were dependent on labels to do it for them. Either by handling it in-house or contracting with a major distributor, labels could get music to consumers in a way that artists simply could not.

86

In fact, just twenty years ago, music distribution involved manufacturing thousands of physical copies of a record, convincing wholesalers and retailers all over the world to stock the record, arranging fleets of trucks and other transportation to get the record to a diverse array of storefronts, maintaining inventory, managing supply chains, and spending big dollars along the way to keep the plan running on all cylinders for months or even years. To call this a financial and logistical nightmare would require a gift for understatement.

Back then, an artist simply couldn't do it alone. They wouldn't have the resources. The extent of an artist-run distribution plan in the old industry would basically be limited to selling CDs out of the trunk of a car. Or, if an artist was really savvy, maybe they could talk a few local record stores into keep a few copies of their music on the shelf to sell on consignment. That was basically all an artist could do on their own. If an artist wanted to do more, they had to sign with a label and give up a big piece of the pie in the process.

But my, oh, my, how things have changed. The Internet has come along and completely obliterated the old distribution model. Online retailers like iTunes and Amazon, as well as music subscription services like Spotify, have supplanted brick-and-mortar storefronts as the way that most consumers get their music. In the world of music retail, digital now dominates physical. And for artists looking for a way to distribute their own music, this is a marvelous development. Digital music distribution means no more manufacturing, no more maintaining inventory, no more trucks, no more supply chain management, and, most importantly, no more need for record labels. Worldwide distribution used to cost hundreds of thousands of dollars. Now it is nearly free, and it is laughably easy to do. Chapter 11 will tell you more about how to effectively and affordably do your own distribution.

Promotion

The aforementioned technological hurricane that hit the music industry has allowed independent artists to make their own records. Moreover, it has allowed them to get those records to their fans just as effectively as any record label can. But there is one more task that must be done to make a successful independent music career: An artist must also be able to let people know that their music exists. This is where promotion comes into play.

Without a strong promotional effort, one's music becomes the proverbial tree falling in the forest with no one around to hear it. And much like recording and distribution, widespread promotion of new releases was once an unaffordable luxury for independent artists. In the pre-hurricane days, promoting a single invariably meant spending big bucks on a radio promotion campaign. Rather than do this sort of promotion in-house, labels usually contracted with outside promotion companies to get an artist's song played on the radio.

These efforts were critical in the old industry. Terrestrial radio was the principal means by which consumers discovered new songs. A failed radio promotion campaign was a kiss of death for a new single, so a lot of money had to be spent on the right promoters to make sure an artist's recordings found their way to the FM dial. This is not to discount other important avenues of promotion, however. Things like music videos, promotional appearances, song placements in various media, and television and print advertising were all important arrows in a label's promotional quiver. If these expensive initiatives were not utilized, new songs could not reach the masses.

As a result, promotional budgets for an artist's label-backed single could go well into the six figures, and even top $1 million! Good luck coming up with that kind of cash as an indie. Time to sign that record deal, right? Because even if you can record and distribute your recordings without a label, you *certainly* can't get those recordings sufficiently promoted without one.

Nonsense! It's a new world now. And to those who think that a high-priced label promotion plan is the only way to move units nowadays, I offer one word of response: Beyoncé.

Why Beyoncé? In December 2013, this pop star/music icon/queen of the universe released her fifth studio album as a solo artist. As one might expect from any of "Queen Bey's" efforts, the self-titled release was a massive success. But what was not expected was the way she promoted the work. Eschewing the traditional means of promoting a top-shelf artist's latest album, Beyoncé's camp decided to do things differently. In the buildup to her December

2013 release, there was no radio airplay, public appearances, TV commercials, promotional music videos, or anything of that nature. There was not even a single released in anticipation of the album. In fact, the release of the album was kept completely secret.

Then, all of a sudden, a Beyoncé LP with 17 accompanying music videos just popped up on iTunes without warning.

Needless to say, the Internet went nuts. People were flabbergasted that the biggest pop star in the world managed to put out an album under cover of darkness. In a matter of hours, every person with a blog or social media account was talking about her latest record. The album generated over one million tweets in its first twelve hours of existence and seemingly every media outlet was talking about her stealth release.

When the dust finally started to settle, the sales figures were bonkers: The album moved 430,000 copies on iTunes in twenty-four hours, cleared 600,000 units within three days, and debuted at the top of the Billboard album charts by the end of the week, netting Beyoncé her fifth consecutive #1 LP. Her album was the best-selling release by a female artist in 2013, even though her record did not even come out until mid-December of that year.

The album's total three-day gross: nearly $10 million.

The album's total pre-release promotion budget: $0.

I am sure there was thunderous celebration at Columbia Records that weekend. As Beyoncé's record label, Columbia profited immensely from their artist's #1 megahit. They made millions off of Beyoncé's album without having to lift a finger during the pre-release. A pretty sweet deal, all things considered. Big money for no effort.

But I like to think that, deep down, amidst all of the hurrahs, money-counting, and back-slapping taking place at the label during that time, some of the folks at Columbia were feeling more mixed emotions.

On one hand: The label just sold a ton of Beyoncé records without having to spend a cent on promotion.

But on the other hand: Beyoncé just sold a ton of records without *needing* her label to spend a cent on promotion.

The implications of this are staggering. Beyoncé did not need Columbia's high-priced marketing operation to get the word out. Instead, a vast expanse of bloggers, news websites, and social media denizens made her album the biggest in the world for free. Columbia Records did not make Beyoncé's album a hit—Twitter did. And the industry will never be the same.

Beyoncé's example shows us that promotion is quickly becoming a different game. The big-ticket world of terrestrial radio campaigns, TV advertising, and late night talk show appearances is giving way to a universe of tweets, likes, YouTube views, blog entries, and other Internet phenomena that can get you worldwide exposure without the bloated budget.

Will it be as simple for you as it was for Beyoncé? Of course not. You are not one of the biggest stars in pop music. If you plop some songs onto iTunes and don't tell anyone about it, you will make a grand total of zero dollars and zero cents (before taxes). Beyoncé has an army of rabid fans who are ready to consume anything she creates at a moment's notice. You (most likely) do not. But with hard work, and effective use of the limitless free promotion the Internet provides, you can build your own assemblage of devoted die-hards and make a living as a musician without a record company taking over your career.

That being said, I am not using the term "hard work" loosely when I talk about promoting your music on the Internet. Worldwide promotion is now free for you, but that also means it is free for everyone. So if you want to cut through the clutter, you will need to hustle and be more creative than your peers. Becoming a success in this world means that you will be spending much more time promoting your music than you will be creating it. Much, much more.

If you're the sort of person who does not feel comfortable with extensive and exhaustive self-promotion, then you'd better get comfortable. Music promotion in the age of social media means that you will need to put yourself out there—every single day. Sites like Facebook and Twitter have made the over-sharing of people's lives the new normal, and have also broken down barriers that existed between entertainers and their fans. This means that music consumers now expect to hear from musicians directly, and they want to hear from them all of the time.

They want to hear about your music, obviously, but they also want to see pictures of you, they want to know what is going on in your life, they want to know how you grew up, they want to know what you had for lunch yesterday, they want to know what music and movies you like, they want to know what conditioner you use to make your locks so bouncy, and much more. You don't have to share everything I just mentioned, but keep in mind that fans want to know everything they can about you, and you'd better be ready to show them who you are—constantly. It's a new promotional world out there, and it does not pay to be shy.

Swimming on Your Own

Thanks to 21ˢᵗ century innovation, today's music industry presents considerably more opportunities for artists like you. And at the risk of getting the score to *Annie Get Your Gun* stuck in your head, I can proclaim that you now live in a world where anything your label can do, you can do better—and cheaper! The hurricane has passed through, the water has seeped in, and there is nothing stopping you from swimming in a limitless ocean.

Go get your fish.

CHAPTER 9

YOUR EMPIRE

Welcome to the new industry!

It has never been more possible for those who create music and those who profit the most from it to be one and the same. The opportunity to break free from typical record labels has a lot of positive implications for you as an artist. It means actually owning the recordings you create, and exploiting them as you wish. It means making money from your music directly, and not merely receiving royalty crumbs after a label has already feasted on your sales. It means holding onto more of your performing and merchandising income, and not giving it away to a company which did nothing to help you obtain said income. Best of all, it means making your own career decisions, and not subjecting your professional life to the whims of a faceless entity.

You're The Boss!

In fact, the current environment is such that artists can now take full control of *every* aspect of their entertainment livelihood. This new music business is shifting towards being one that is artist-centered, and not label-centered. The most successful artists will be the ones who can expertly manage all of the aspects of their music career. This includes the jobs that labels commonly do—such as the recording, distribution, and promotion activities discussed in the previous chapter—but it also means performing well in a variety of other areas.. Areas like publishing, booking, merchandising, business administration, financing, and much more are all yours to manage in a way that is best for you.

There is something inherently invigorating about being at the top of your entertainment pyramid and answering to no one. After all, who doesn't want to be their own boss? C.T. Fields, musician and member of Pittsburgh-based indie band Lovebettie expresses this sentiment quite well: "Record labels have collapsed, and artists need to ask themselves now whether they want to be the cowboy, or whether they want to be the cattle. I personally want to be the cowboy, the entrepreneur making their own way, instead of waiting for someone to fit me into a mold."

Running Your Empire

But as exciting as it sounds to don your Stetson, hop on your hoss, and take full control of your career, it is also understandable if this might all seem a little overwhelming to you. "I am an artist, not an entrepreneur," you might say. "Creating and performing music is hard enough. I can't also be expected to run my own business, craft my own brand, promote and distribute my own music, create and sell my own merchandise, book my own performances, review my own contracts, fund my own projects, and keep my own books! I just don't have the expertise to do all of these things. It is impossible for me to be a do-it-yourself ("DIY") artist."

You Can Learn

Let's take a moment and look at those last two sentences more closely. These are the two most common statements I hear from artists who are skeptical that they can run their own entertainment empires. We'll start with the first one. To those who tell me that they cannot run their own careers because they don't know *how* to manage their own support services, my response is simple: You can learn.

None of this is beyond your reach. You don't need any sort of specialized education or training to administer your career. You just need to get a handle on some of the basic aspects of running an entertainment organization. The subsequent chapters of this book will help you with that. By applying the principles outlined in the ensuing pages, you can effectively run every part of your professional life—be it promotion, fundraising, merchandising, business management, or other areas.

You Don't Have to Do Everything

Now, to the second point. When I tell musicians that they are capable of running their own operation, they will tell me that it is simply impossible for them to "do everything themselves." They will claim that there are not enough hours in the day for them to run the business side of their careers and still create music. Moreover, they will argue that there are some business tasks that they simply lack the formal education to perform, like handling legal documents. In short, they tell me, it is naïve to think that one can become successful as a DIY musician.

To which I respond: "Who said anything about being a DIY musician?" Musicians who make the "You can't expect me to do everything myself" argument are confusing "running" your business with "doing everything" for your business. In a popular blog post describing her successful music career, NYC-based indie artist Kim Boekbinder expressed this point expertly, writing,

> When the Internet paved the way for more musicians to go it on their own without a record label and traditional management, the term [DIY] got more usage. But today the term "DIY" is a lie . . . . I don't call myself "DIY." I am an artist, making art, and doing whatever I need to do to reach my fans. I do a lot of things myself, but my fans help me, my friends help me, and the people I hire help me a lot . . . . No business is built by one person alone.

Let's Talk Some More About Delegating

Like nearly all successful entrepreneurs, you will obviously need people to help you along the way. To achieve your entertainment industry goals, you might need an administrator to handle your publishing, agents to help book gigs, and publicists to get the word out on your big projects. You might need lawyers from time to time to review contracts and keep your business activities above board. You might need an accountant one day if your finances become too complex to manage on your own. And who knows: You might even get to the point in your career where you need to bring in a manager to run the day-to-day operations of your empire.

The Three Fs

In addition to all of the above, you will also need the help of the three most important groups of all, which I call the "Three Fs": Friends, Family, and Fans. Making the most of your Three Fs is critical to getting your career off the ground in its early stages. These people are your heart and soul. They can provide you all sorts of

94

services. Moreover, their support tends to be zealous, everlasting, and (most importantly) inexpensive. Whether it is the CPA uncle providing you cut-rate accounting services, or the superfan letting you crash on his couch when you perform in his hometown, I cannot overstate the importance of having a lot of these people in your life.

General Rules for Delegating

So don't worry: Just because you are independent does not mean you are alone. Just like in the label-centered model, there will be others around to help you achieve your ambitions. The difference is that, in this artist-centered model, you have true control over who those others are and how they do their job. This allows you to make your own career decisions and, since you are the true boss, keep more of what you earn.

The later chapters will provide plenty of advice on when and how to outsource certain of the various aspects of your business to other people or companies. When you are starting out, you will do more things yourself since you will have neither the need nor the resources to have others do them for you. Over time, this will change. Your career will become more complex, your bank account will become more accommodating, and delegation will become more prudent. While more specific discussion of this topic is saved for later, there are two general points on outsourcing worth bringing up now:

Rule #1: If you are not good at something, delegate it

It is a fundamental business principle that successful organizations tend to outsource activities that are unrelated to their core competencies. In other words, if they are not good at something, they have someone else do it for them. This allows the organization to invest more of its time and resources in whatever activity it does best. The same goes for you as an artist-entrepreneur. If you are not good at a particular activity, have someone else who is good at it do it for you. This will give you more time to focus on the things you do well. Or, as Kim Boekbinder so expertly puts it: "Know your strengths. Do those things. Know your weaknesses. Don't do those things."

If you happen to be good at crunching numbers and handling money, then there's no need to get a business manager in the early stages of your career. Are you good at video editing? Then save money by putting together your own music videos and YouTube clips. Conversely, if you are not good at graphic design, then find someone else to make your logos and artwork. If you don't know the first thing about getting your music onto movies and TV shows, then enlist the services of a song plugging organization.

As your organization grows, you may find that the things you were once "good enough" to do yourself are now beyond your expertise or simply no longer worth your time. When that happens, you will need to delegate those things, too. Booking your own gigs might have been doable when all you needed to do was network with local club owners. But when you find yourself upgrading to bigger venues and expanding your geographic area, you will be well served by using a professional booking agent in lieu of self-booking. No matter how good you are at convincing venues to give you a date, it will be a better use of your resources to have an agent do this work for you once you get big enough.

One final point on this subject: Before you decide that you are "not good" at something and try to outsource it, make sure that you read through the lessons in the remainder of this book. The purpose of the upcoming chapters is to give you a strong grounding in the basic aspects of running your own entertainment organization. It will discuss concepts such as promotion, publishing, fundraising, recording, distribution, merchandising, legal issues, and much more. Hopefully, after internalizing the information presented in those chapters, you will be in a much better position to do more things on your own—at least in the early stages of your career. This will save you a lot of money early on.

Rule #2. You can compensate those you help you in any way you like…except one.

A lot of your supporting cast members, despite the various functions they serve, have one thing in common: They will not work for free. I say "a lot" and not "all," however, because you might luck out and get some sweetheart deals from people in your Three Fs.

Maybe you have a lawyer sister willing to review your contracts pro bono, for example (If so, lucky you!).

But, aside from those more fortuitous arrangements, the other people and businesses that do things for your career will need to be paid. There are a wide variety of ways to compensate those who help advance your livelihood. Some of them you will pay in a straight, one-time cash payment. You will take care of a lot of your simple expenditures this way: A bass player plays at your gig for one night and you send him some cash. You use Paypal to forward a sum to a writer who crafts a killer bio for your electronic press kit. You write a painfully large check to a PR firm to help give your next big project some serious promotional "oomph." Whatever you are paying for under this method, the transaction is almost always quick and uncomplicated.

You can also use non-cash transactions to get certain services. Perhaps some of your die-hards will help set up your stage for a gig in exchange for free drinks (be sure to "pay" them afterwards—you don't want drunk people around your equipment). Or maybe you get a fledgling filmmaker to make your music video in exchange for letting her use some of your songs in her next movie for free. These sorts of transactions are a great way to get important tasks done on the cheap, and sometimes they can even be a great networking opportunity. For example, lots of upstart musicians will perform on a fellow artist's record in exchange for that artist returning the favor for them down the road. As a result, both artists save money in making their record while fostering a valuable connection with a fellow performer that they can later use to their benefit.

Once your operation becomes more sophisticated, you might even have some people you pay on some kind of regular salary or per-event basis. Backup musicians, roadies, assistants, or accountants are all people that you may very well find yourself paying at a more-or-less consistent clip. Obviously, these arrangements tend to be more complicated than just paying for something once. They involve you having to foster ongoing relationships with people and institutions that will have a significant impact on your professional life. Plus, if you are hiring employees, you will wind up confronting a variety of legal and tax issues which are simply the cost of doing business for having support personnel at your beck and call.

Finally, you might pay for some of your entertainment services not with money you have at the time, but with money you will get *later* as a result of the service provided. For example, if you get someone to help with your publishing, you will likely pay them a percentage of the royalties collected when your compositions are exploited. Similarly, if you want a manager to help run your career, this person might want a percentage of the income generated by your career in exchange for their services. Lawyers sometimes work on this basis as well: Some will take a piece of a revenue-generating deal they help close for you in lieu of receiving an up-front retainer or hourly fee.

There is a lot to like about these arrangements. For one thing, they give the service provider a particularly strong incentive to do a good job for you, being that your success means their success. Plus, the contingent aspect of the model allows you to obtain some big-ticket items (like publishing, managerial, and legal services) with no up-front payments and little cost to you in the event that the project in question fails.

This is not to say that there aren't some downsides to this payment method. While this approach protects your wallet in the event of project failure, it may also cost you a big chunk of money if your project succeeds and your service provider takes their cut from a large pie. Moreover, given the difficulties of calculating commissions, it is almost a certainty that you will have a payment dispute with one of your service providers at some point. When this happens, the best case scenario is a series of combative back-and-forth e-mails between you and your servicer. These discussions will usually feature thinly-veiled accusations of stealing coming from both sides. The worst case scenario, of course, is ending up in a courtroom to settle the matter, at which point the accusations of stealing will no longer be so thinly-veiled.

These drawbacks aside, getting entertainment services through contingency payments can be a good thing in many cases. In fact, all of the above payment methods are perfectly reasonable ways to get the services you need but might not be able to do for yourself. Artists with successful careers will use all of these methods at some point. As long as the terms are fair, feel free to pay your service providers with straight cash, straight non-cash, regular payments, or contingent payments however you see fit.

In fact, there is only one payment method that you should avoid at all costs. Holding on to this one asset can make the difference between career success and collapse—financial riches versus ruin. I want you to repeat the following phrase a thousand times, write it down over and over on a sheet a paper, and perhaps even have it tattooed backwards on your body so that you will see it in the mirror when you wake up every morning—it is *that* important:

"I WILL NOT, UNDER ANY CIRCUMSTANCES, GIVE UP MY COPYRIGHTS."

Don't do it. Don't do it. Don't do it. Never, ever, *ever* give even a portion of your intellectual property in exchange for services. Ever. You should sooner sell the bones in your body before you give up any of your copyrights. That includes the copyrights to the songs you write as well as the master rights to recordings of those songs. Do not sell the copyrights you have or the copyrights to the songs or recordings you will make in the future. Don't. Sell. Them. Ever.

Don't Sell Your Copyrights to Get the Services Your Empire Needs

The importance of this point cannot be overstated, so let's discuss it in greater detail. Plenty of companies will want your IP in exchange for doing business with you. As noted in Chapter 4, record labels want complete ownership of all sound recordings you will create as a condition for signing you.

"Why is this a bad thing?" you might ask. At first glance, such an arrangement might sound pretty sweet. Assigning your copyrights to get publishing services, for example, could seem like a good way to get a valuable item without having to pay any money up front. This type of misunderstanding is common because you might not immediately perceive the value of something that is not a tangible piece of property. Not being able to physically see or touch a legal right can make it hard to see its worth. That might make it easy to justify giving up some of those rights to advance your career.

Do not succumb to that line of thinking. In actuality, your copyrights—in every song you write and every recording you create—are the most valuable assets you have in your entertainment operation *by far*. Your copyrights are so insanely valuable that, if you sell any part of them, you are almost assuredly getting ripped off in the transaction—regardless of the value of the service you are receiving in return.

Sell the Milk

Here's why: Think of your music career as a dairy farm and your song and recording copyrights are the cows. Your copyrights generate all of the "milk" that makes the farm profitable. If you don't have enough cows, you won't make enough money over time to keep your farm. Your copyrights are what give you the exclusive right to make copies of your music, make your recordings into music videos, let others perform your songs in public, put your recordings in movies and TV shows, and engage in a wide variety of other profitable activities with your works. Thus, your copyrights are the assets that will generate the most money for you in your career, and they keep generating money for long after you are done making music. They are the lifeblood of your music career.

If you sell one of your cows, you are not just giving up an animal, you are giving up all of the milk that animal will generate for as long as it lives. And in the music world, the cows live for a *really* long time. Under U.S. Copyright law, each copyright you have will last for your entire life plus seventy years. Consequently, you are giving up what could be a tremendous amount of future earnings by selling a copyright.

Moreover, it is a fairly common occurrence in the music business that your copyright cows will make cows of their own at some point, each of which can similarly produce milk for decades. One of the exclusive rights within a copyright is the right to create a "derivative work" based on a previous work. An example of a derivative work would be a music video you made from one of the songs you wrote. The derivative work is itself a copyrighted work which can generate more money for you. This means that if you gave up your cow, you not only lost all of the milk that cow could generate, but you also lost all of the *cows* that cow could generate. Generally speaking, it is not a prudent business strategy to sell any income-producing asset that itself can produce income-producing assets.   ·

So here is the rule to follow when it comes to buying the services you need as an artist: <u>Don't sell the cow; sell the milk instead</u>. In other words, use your copyrights to generate funds, and use those funds to buy the things you need for your career—but do not sell the copyrights themselves. Keep the income-producing asset, and instead spend the income that asset produces.

When I give artists this advice, they usually ask me about a grey area between keeping the asset and spending the income. They want to know about situations where a service provider wants a set percentage of the income their copyrights generate for a set period of time. Basically, the service provider wants a certain portion of the cow's milk for a limited period.

This is perfectly fine (provided that the specific terms are fair), since you are still retaining full control and ownership over the copyright. All you are doing is selling the milk in this scenario. The buyer does not get a perpetual right to your income as it would if you sold a part of the cow itself. Their income rights will last only as long as your agreement with the provider lasts.

In fact, this is a great way to do business with publishing administrators. In a typical deal, you would give that company a percentage (10-15% or so) of the income your songs produce in exchange for the administrator handling your song publishing. This is no different than the "contingency payment" model discussed earlier. It is a perfectly reasonable way to obtain this valuable service, provided that you get fair terms on the deal itself.

This method is in stark contrast to another common method of handling song publishing: the so-called "co-publishing" deal. With a co-publishing deal, a publishing company will manage your song copyrights in exchange for co-ownership of the copyright and usually a 25% share of the songs' income. While co-publishing agreements are common in the music industry, they should generally be avoided by artists trying to build their careers. Why? Because they involve selling the cow, instead of selling the milk. As a

101

result, publishing administration deals are preferable to co-publishing deals. No service is valuable enough that it warrants selling your income-producing assets.

Building Your Empire

The rest of this book will outline specific strategies for building your own entertainment empire. While you will certainly depend on many others to achieve your success, you will be the undisputed leader of your operation. The next chapter will discuss the initial steps you must take to help structure your career. Each subsequent chapter will then provide valuable information for running your organization effectively in every aspect of the music business. By internalizing the lessons of these chapters, you will be in a strong position to achieve success on your own terms. These lessons will help you become the artist-entrepreneur you want to be, free from the suffocating influence of record companies or any other organization that would take your copyrights, control your creative and business endeavors, and devour your earnings.

CHAPTER 10
MAKE A PLAN

Don't Skip This Simple Step

There is one thing you absolutely *must* do in order to create a thriving independent music operation. Many artists ignore this task, and they do so at their peril. Taking this action is more vital to your music career's success than years of guitar lessons or booking a bunch of large-venue gigs. If you do this task effectively, you'll be more successful and achieve your success sooner. But if you skip it, you could wind up spinning your wheels and wasting much of your time and talent.

And here is the good news about this thing you must do: It is actually quite easy to do. It won't cost you a dime and you won't even have to leave your couch or break a sweat to do it. In fact, after reading this chapter, you can do this task right now and probably finish in a few hours, tops. What you need to do, right now and before you take any other major steps with your music, is make a plan for your career.

Starting an undertaking as complicated as an entertainment career requires that you have a concrete plan for how you will run your operation. If you want to succeed, you need to have a plan. To quote the ancient Chinese military philosopher Sun Tzu: "The general who wins a battle makes many calculations in his temple ere the battle is fought. The general who loses a battle makes but few calculations beforehand."

As you get your music career off the ground, there will be a lot of moving parts for you to coordinate. You will need an effective plan to keep things moving and make sure all aspects of your career are working toward a common goal. A career plan will also help you make the most of your limited resources (e.g., money, talents, and personnel) in furtherance of your ambitions.

Remember: You are not just trying to make some music; you are trying to run an entertainment company that could potentially be worth millions someday. Few multi-million dollar ventures in any industry have come about without a good business plan, and your venture will be no exception. Even if you have worked in the business for many years and have already made some money, you still need to make a plan. There is no time like the present to give your career a strong sense of direction.

Putting together a business plan may sound like an annoying first step—an unnecessary waste of paper that just gets in the way of all the creative stuff you could be doing with that time instead. "I write songs, not career plans," I hear you saying. "Don't waste my time with this menial crap." You might even argue that you got into music specifically to avoid the sort of corporate, white-collar scut work that writing a career plan seems to exemplify.

If that is how you feel, then I should tell you this, now, at the outset: If this is the livelihood you want, get used to doing corporate white-collar scut work. It will be much of your life from here on. Learn to love it, or at least tolerate it. Creating your own music operation means doing lots of paperwork. Being successful in the artist-driven music industry means assuming your role as a businessperson and accepting all of the paper pushing that comes with it. In your career, you will be writing as many documents as you will chord progressions, recording as much ledger data on spreadsheets as you will vocal takes in a studio. A business plan is just one of the many administrative undertakings you will have to assume to run your empire. Be ready to do these things and do them well.

Besides, as a musician, you already plan out big projects all of the time before you do them. You likely spend hours crafting the perfect set list for an important gig. You probably make careful budgets before you start any big spending projects. When you are about to go into an expensive studio to record, I imagine you plot out your time very carefully so that you can get the most bang for your buck out of this costly activity. If you are willing to plan for all of those events in your career, surely you can take a little time to plan for your career as a whole.

And if you follow the steps outlined in this chapter, making the plan will be easy—and quite satisfying. Engaging in this exercise will help you see a clearer path between where you are now and where you want to be as an artist. It will provide invaluable guidance on the long journey ahead. It will allow you to make the most of every resource you have, and even reveal additional resources that you didn't know you had.

Whenever an aspiring musician approaches me and asks, "How do I get started with my career?" I always tell them to complete the career plan steps which I outline in this chapter. I even share these steps with all of the artists I work with in my legal practice. In fact, I have come to find that having a client sit down and map out their career strategy is far more valuable to them than any legal advice I will provide.

So, without further ado, here are the four steps you need to take to plan out your artist-driven music operation:

Step 1: Make Sure You Are Ready

The first step you must make in your career plan is to make sure that you are actually ready for this career. The advice contained in this book will only be useful to the extent that you are ready to be a professional artist in the music industry. So before you move forward on this path, you must make sure that you are.

Do You Have the Time?

The first part of being "ready" is making sure that you have the time to give your music career the attention it deserves. The music industry is a time-consuming enterprise, one that will gobble up many hours of your life. Moreover, the hours it takes from you tend to be highly-valued ones—evening and weekend hours when you might otherwise be resting or spending time with friends and family. These are the hours you will work because these are the hours when people want to go out and enjoy music. When I want to hang out with my musician friends, I have resigned myself to scheduling meetups with them at weird times of the week (like Tuesday afternoons and Sunday mornings). Friday and Saturday nights? Not a chance. They are on the clock. You will never see my musician friends at a Saturday night party—unless of course they are playing at the party.

Does this mean you have to immediately quit your job to start the next phase of your music career? No. In fact, having the income stream of a full-time job can help you fund your music in the early stages. Eventually, your music career could reach the point where you will have to quit your job and focus on your art fully, but it is possible to balance both gigs, at least during your career's infancy.

If you do keep your day job (by day: mild-mannered systems analyst, by night: rock demigod), be ready for a brutal life schedule. Your music career will be another full-time job for you (and then some). You will work insane hours and travel a lot. Strongly consider whether you have the time for such an undertaking at this stage in your life.

Here are some questions to consider in that regard:

- Does your day job have particularly long hours?
- Are the hours unpredictable such that it would be hard for you schedule performance gigs in advance?
- Do you have to work nights and weekends frequently in your job?
- Do you have any non-work obligations or hobbies that you cannot stop doing?
- Are you the primary caregiver for a child or other loved one?
- Do you have any personal issues or significant health problems that would prevent you from being able to give your music your full attention?

To be clear: Just because you answered "Yes" to any of the above questions does not necessarily mean that you should give up on your music career. There are plenty of people with busy schedules, children to raise, or other personal obstacles who still manage to make it work. Besides, if you have some of these difficulties and still manage to succeed, I don't want you excoriating me in some Grammy acceptance speech five years from now ("And to that stupid lawyer Ryan Kairalla who said in his book that I would never make it because I have two kids... Look at me now, jerk!").

I only present the above questions to help you make a prudent decision and balance your current obligations with your future ambitions. If you find that you do have a lot of non-music things going on in your life, see if there are ways that you can lighten that load to give you more time for your art. Perhaps you can ask your boss for a more predictable work schedule or you can enlist the help of supportive family and friends to help you handle any personal obligations you might have. Maybe you'll have to give up on your other hobbies for the sake of furthering your music.

If you are part of a band, it is also important for you to ensure that all of your band members are similarly free of significant personal obligations before you start or continue a career with them. An artist I have spoken with on this subject, himself a member of an acclaimed indie rock band, told me that his group has frequently replaced members who "got married, had kids, had very clingy relationships, got into drugs, had a crazy job" or had any other personal issues significant enough to keep them from keeping up with the band's extensive touring schedule. If these issues exist with a band member, this artist noted, "it is just not going to work and you have to let that person go. You have to be honest about it no matter how much you like or love that person."

Do You Have the Talent?

Next, you have to determine whether you have the requisite musical talent to succeed in this business. Nothing in this book will teach you how to sing, write songs, or perform in front of others. I assume that you can already do those things and do them *really, really* well. If you can't, you need to take a step back first and get your skills to where they need to be.

Acclaimed indie singer-songwriter Rachael Sage echoes this sentiment. A twenty-year industry veteran with her own successful entertainment company, Sage encourages new artists to slow down and hone their craft before trying to break into the business. "The key in this business is being ready," she implores. "Making big jumps in your career before you are ready is like pushing an actor out on stage who hasn't memorized their lines yet." Sage notes that advancement opportunities for artists can be rare, and they need to be ready to make the most of each one. "Do the work and make an investment in yourself, so when the opportunity comes to go on tour as the opener for an artist you love, they don't just give you one gig, they see you and want to give you ten."

Before making big career moves, Sage recommends artists find welcoming, supportive environments to improve their skills and find their unique voice as an artist. "Find a regular gig, a regular, low-pressure kind of residency where you can share and experiment and really grow." An aspiring professional needs to make songwriting and performance practice a regular part of each day, much like daily physical exercise. Spend a lot of time at open mic nights, coffee shops, and small local venues to cultivate your sound. Join or start a musicians' or songwriters' club/cooperative in your hometown. These organizations can help you boost your skills, get honest peer feedback, and network with others in your field. You can use websites like meetup.com to look for existing cooperatives or to advertise one you created.

At this point, you might be asking, "Well, how do I *know* if I'm talented enough?" It is a reasonable question to ask: How much talent is enough? And how can one measure something that has an element of subjectivity to it? Unfortunately, I can't offer a simple answer to this question. Some would say, "If you even have to ask if your music is good enough, it likely isn't." While that may be true in some cases, it is also true that even the most celebrated performers have self-doubt in their abilities from time to time. Don't let your own insecurities keep you from achieving your dreams.

Others have introduced methods of their own to answer this question. In his wildly-popular book *All You Need to Know About the Music Business*, entertainment lawyer Donald Passman says that if you truly believe in your "gut" that you are ready for a professional career, then you are. I believe that Passman's standard does have some accuracy to it. I happen to be a big proponent of adhering to gut feelings in many situations. In fact, there is actually quite a bit of science supporting the practice of making decisions based on one's gut (or intuition, or hunches—whatever you want to call it). A lot of times, your gut will be right on the money.

That being said, I also believe that, when it comes to evaluating your musical talent, there are a lot of times when your gut can be a damned liar. For evidence of this, look no further than the scores of tone-deaf American Idol contestants who annually subject TV viewers to their abhorrent auditions. At some point, all of these ghastly crooners must have fallen victim to an untrustworthy gut—

one which somehow managed to convince them that they were destined to win a nationwide singing competition.

Indeed, "Am I talented enough?" is a critically-important question for any artist to answer before they embark on a career in music. Succeeding in this industry is challenging enough even for the very best, and so the importance of having truly exceptional abilities cannot be overstated. In short, just being "talented enough" is, in fact, not talented enough.

Moreover, having enough talent is more than just being really, really good at music. There are plenty of highly-skilled performers out there whose creative product never resonates with a significant segment of the public. Having a lot of ability is a necessary requirement for success, but it is not all you need. Your talent also has to be *distinctive*. Your offering has to be unique, such that consumers can distinguish you from the infinite expanse of music available to them. If you look and sound like everything else out there, then you will never cut through the clutter. If you have amazing talent but not *distinctive* talent, then you need to spend time crafting your own unique look, sound, and musical personality.

I know you may be looking for an easy standard or test to see if you have the right kind of abilities to succeed. But if there is such a test out there, I, unfortunately, have not heard of it. There is no simple definition of that "it" quality that a performer needs to become a star. However, to help aid you in answering that question for yourself, I can provide several helpful tips that successful artists have relayed to me in the past:

- Seek the honest opinion of a successful music professional. This can be a musician, music critic, or perhaps an industry executive. It just needs to be someone with a pedigree that makes them seem likely to know what they are talking about. Make sure this is someone you trust, but not someone who is too close to you (like a close friend or family member). It is critical to get an unbiased assessment. Ask for their complete, brutal honesty. Be sure to get straight answers from this person by asking them clear questions, such as: (1) Do you think I have enough talent to succeed in the music industry? (2) Do you think my creative product is distinctive enough to be memorable to others?

- After you talk to that person, find another successful music professional and seek their opinion as well. To figure out something this important, it is definitely worth it to get a second (and perhaps a third and fourth) opinion. One person's assessment (be it positive or negative) should not be taken as gospel. Having a larger sample size of experts evaluating your abilities will give you a more accurate picture of where you are in your artistic development.

- Ask yourself whether your music and performances get a highly-positive reception from listeners who are not your family and friends. Are people you've never met sharing your YouTube videos with others? Are a lot of strangers coming to your shows? Do you already have a lot of fans of your music on social media sites that are not friends of yours?

- Ask yourself whether you have received serious interest from a record label or other similar entertainment company. Obviously, you should not sign with said label (and if you are seriously asking "Why not?" then you *really* need to go back and read the first nine chapters all over again). However, the interest you receive from such a company can be a good indication that you might have what it takes to achieve stardom.

- Look at the reputation you currently have as a musician in your hometown. Oftentimes, "conquering" your local area as a musician indicates that you have the skill set to spread your art into other cities' music scenes.

Before we move on, I have one last note on this subject. It is entirely possible that, even after putting in a ton of time to hone your craft, you may *never* have the talent to succeed in the music business. Unfortunately, some will never have what it takes to be an elite-level musical talent—no matter how much they practice (as anyone who has heard my guitar playing can attest).

If you follow the above advice and discover that you simply don't have the innate gifts needed to hit the big time, do not despair. The time you have spent in music has not been time wasted. There is still significant value to making music a part of your life even if you do not become a star performer. Countless studies have revealed innumerable benefits to engaging in music as a hobby. These benefits include everything from lowering stress levels to improving reasoning skills and memory, as well as increasing self-confidence. Therefore, even if you do not make a career out of music performance, you can feel good knowing that the time you have already spent in this field will undoubtedly make you a happier and more successful human being.

Step 2: Take Inventory of Your Strengths and Weaknesses

After determining that you've "got the goods" for a career in music, it is time to move on to the next step in developing your career plan. This step will involve you identifying all of the strengths and weaknesses of your music operation as it currently exists. If you want to make effective strategic decisions for your music career, you need to first know all of the weapons you have at your disposal. And, of equal importance, you need to know all of your vulnerabilities. This act of "taking career inventory" will ensure that you make decisions that play to your positives and work around your negatives.

When evaluating your strengths and weaknesses, it is important to not only look at your internal strengths and weaknesses, but also to look at how your external environment will affect your career both positively and negatively. Those of you out there who took business classes in school might be thinking that the above sounds a lot like a SWOT analysis. A SWOT analysis is a popular strategic planning exercise that business organizations use to help evaluate potential ventures. It involves an organization identifying its **S**trengths (internal characteristics that are advantages to the organization), **W**eaknesses (internal characteristics that are disadvantages to the organization), **O**pportunities (external factors that the organization can use to its advantage), and **T**hreats (external factors that could disadvantage the organization) in attempting to achieve a business objective.

Rare is the organization that undertakes a significant project without first identifying their "SWOTs." It is an effective way to take stock of one's business landscape before plunging into a particular venture. Since your music career is itself a massive business project,

111

engaging in a similar exercise will be one of the smartest things you can do for your livelihood. The process outlined in this book, however, will be slightly different from a traditional SWOT analysis. To make things a little simpler, we will combine the **S**trengths and **O**pportunities part of a SWOT analysis into a section called "My Strengths" and we will combine the **W**eaknesses and **T**hreats part into a section called "My Weaknesses."

Here is how this exercise will work: First, take two sheets of paper. You will split each paper into two columns. The right column should be wider than the left column. Label the top of the left-hand column of the first paper "My Strengths" and the top of the left-hand column of the second paper "My Weaknesses." Next, you will list all of your internal and external strengths your music operation will have in the first left-hand column and all of your internal and external weaknesses in the other left-hand column. Your papers should look like Figure A.

Figure A

My Strengths

My Weaknesses

To fill in each left-hand column, you need to identify the Strengths and Weaknesses of your music operation. Basically, you need to determine what advantages and disadvantages you will face in trying to build your career. What tools will you have to help you climb the mountain, and what are the things that will weigh you down? Depending on how thorough you are (and the more thorough, the better) you will likely need multiple sheets for your Strengths and Weaknesses.

A big part of the value of this exercise comes from uncovering strengths and weaknesses of which you were previously unaware. Your resources are limited, so you need to make the most of every asset you have as well as be able to see all of your hidden obstacles. Therefore, to help you find more of your organization's positives and negatives, consider the questions provided below. These questions will ask you about every facet of your entertainment venture. And depending on whether you answer these questions favorably or unfavorably, you will gain insight as to what things you can put in each of the two left-hand columns. While this long list of career questions might be exhausting to read, it is by no means exhaustive. You will likely be able to come up with additional strengths and weaknesses not addressed by these questions.

For ease of organization, the questions have been divided into six different sections, each of which corresponds to a different area of an independent artist's entertainment operation:

Content Creation and Distribution

1. Do you have any good-quality audio recordings of your music already available (or soon to be available) to the public?
2. Do you have easy and low-cost access to any music recording and editing equipment? If so, what is the level of sophistication of this equipment? Is it a simple home setup? Is it a high-level recording studio?
3. Do you have any experience and/or knowledge regarding producing recorded music? If not, do you have low-cost and easy access to someone who does?
4. Do you have any music engineering, editing, mixing, or mastering experience and/or knowledge? If not, do you have easy and low-cost access to someone who does?

115

5. Do you have unusually high skill at a particular musical instrument? Can you play multiple musical instruments?

6. Do you have an unusually good singing voice for the style of music that you do? Is there something distinctive about your singing voice?

7. Do you play in a band, or at least have strong relationships with a number of musicians in your area, that would be willing to play on your projects for low cost?

8. Are you a good graphic/visual artist such that you can design your own artwork for your recordings? If not, do you have easy and low-cost access to someone who does?

9. Are you familiar with the various methods to distribute recordings, both physical and digital? Have you used these methods before? Do you currently distribute your music in a wide variety of ways?

10. Do you have any completed good-quality video recordings of your music (e.g., videos of your live performances, music videos, or "unplugged" sessions)?

11. Do you have easy and low-cost access to any video recording and editing equipment? If so, what is the level of sophistication of this equipment? Is it something more common, like a smartphone or basic editing software, or do you have access to more professional-level recording technology (e.g., professional camera, microphones, or lighting, and professional editing software)?

12. Do you have any experience and/or knowledge regarding directing videos? If not, do you have low-cost and easy access to someone who does?

13. Do you have any video editing experience and/or knowledge? If not, do you have easy and low-cost access to someone who does?

14. Are you good at creating interesting and engaging storyboards for music videos?

Song Publishing

15. Do you write many of your own songs?

16. Are you able to write a lot of songs quickly, or is songwriting a slower process for you?

17. Do you currently have a lot of completed, good-quality songs that you have written?

18. Have some of the songs you have written been made into recordings (recorded by you or by others)?

19. Have some of the songs you have written been used for non-record purposes (such as for use by TV shows, video games, movies, or advertisements)?

20. Are the songs you write particularly well-suited for non-record purposes (such as for use by TV shows, video games, movies, or advertisements)?

21. Have you already set up any arrangements to help monetize your songs, such as with a publishing administrator or a song plugger? If not, are you currently in a position to build the necessary relationships to create those arrangements?

Promotion

22. Have you crafted a strong "brand" for yourself? In other words, have you built a distinct identity as a performer that allows you to connect with specific segments of music consumers?

23. Is there a particular segment of the public with whom your music resonates particularly strongly? This segment can be an age group, fans of a certain genre, fans of a particular nationality, a certain lifestyle group, or any other group identifiable by common attributes.

24. Do you have a good-quality logo for yourself? If not, do you have the graphic design skills to create one or do you have easy and low-cost access to someone who does?

25. Do you have a promotional bio for yourself? If not, do you have the writing skills to create an engaging promotional bio or do you have easy and low-cost access to someone who does?

26. Do you have an interesting life story that would particularly engage the public?

27. Do you have a high-quality website for your career? If not, do you have the web design skills to create one or do you have easy and low-cost access to someone who does?

28. Do you have easy and low-cost access to any high-quality photography equipment?

29. Do you have easy and low-cost access to a good photographer?

30. Are you outgoing when it comes to promoting yourself? Are you shy about "putting yourself out there," or do you have little difficulty exposing who you are to others through various types of media?

31. Are you good at coming up with interesting promotional ideas for your music?

32. Do you currently have a long mailing list?

33. Are you savvy with multiple forms of social media? To answer, "Yes," to this question, you must, at a minimum, be savvy with Twitter, Facebook, and Instagram.

34. Do you currently use social media significantly for your career?

35. Do you currently have a strong following for your career (both in terms of the quantity and engagement of your following) on any of your social media pages?

36. Review your answer to question 11. Does your answer suggest that you have the equipment necessary to make promotional videos of yourself for YouTube and your social media pages?

37. Are you good at blogging?

38. Are you good at vlogging?

39. Are you good at podcasting? Do you have access to podcasting equipment?

40. Do you have any particularly strong non-music talents? This would include nearly *anything* that might be of interest to your fans: writing poetry, writing novels, painting, drawing, sculpture, fashion design, cooking, photography, martial arts, juggling, magic tricks, knitting, woodworking, skateboarding, origami, etc. Again, almost anything works for this question.

41. Do you have any particularly strong non-music interests that you could share with your fans?

42. Do you currently have relationships with any people or organizations that work in areas related to music promotion (e.g., independent promoters, publicists, or music blog editors)?

43. Do you currently have relationships with musicians or other entertainers who would be willing to help you promote your career? Are these musicians more famous than you or would at least give you access to different segments of fans?

44. Do you currently have relationships with any other professionals who could help promote your career?

Live Performances

45. Are you able to perform your music comfortably in front of a live audience?

46. Are you an unusually good live performer?

47. Are you currently at a stage in your life where you have the energy and health to perform gigs on a regular basis? Can you perform every weekend? How about multiple times a week?

48. Are your work/school/family obligations flexible enough that you tend to have a high level of availability for gigs?

49. Are your live performances particularly distinctive in any way (outside of your skill as a performer)?

50. Do you live in a town that has a good live music scene? Are there lots of places for a musician of your genre and career stage to play?

51. Do you have strong connections with other musicians in your town (or elsewhere) such that you can learn of and attain performance opportunities from those other musicians?

52. Are you already performing regularly in your local area? Regionally? Nationally?

53. Do you currently have relationships with any people or organizations that work in areas related to booking live performances (e.g., booking agents, promoters, or venue owners)?

54. Do you have access to transportation that allows you to easily perform in areas far from where you reside?

55. Does your transportation allow you to easily transport the equipment you would need for your live performances?

Fundraising and Merchandising

56. Do you have a lot of personal wealth or have any wealthy family members who are willing to help support your career?

57. Do you have a large base of friends and family who are highly supportive of your career and are ready and willing to help your career in non-financial ways?

58. Do you have any existing recordings or songs that are generating income for you?

59. Are you already generating considerable income from your live performances?

60. Do you have relationships with musicians or other individuals that you can utilize to obtain some of the things you need via non-cash transactions? An example of this would be getting a local musician to play on one of your recordings in exchange for you playing on one of theirs.

61. Do you have any experience with using crowdfunding websites like Kickstarter or GoFundMe?

62. Do you currently sell any merchandise? Do you have a wide variety of merchandise?

63. Do you sell this merchandise at your live shows? Do you sell it on the Internet?

64. Are you good at creating designs and concepts for common merchandise items (e.g., T-shirts, hats, stickers, or posters)?

65. Are you good at coming up with interesting ideas for merchandise to sell? Are you good at coming up with merchandise ideas that particularly resonate with a specific segment of your audience?

66. Are you good at making some kind of unique item or product that you could sell as merchandise to your fans (e.g., original artwork, poetry books, or clothing)?

Business Operations

67. Are you good at keeping accounting books for your career operations?

68. Do you have a qualified close friend or family member who is willing to provide you with low-cost accounting services?

69. Are you good at handling your own low-level legal issues (forming legal entities, registering copyrights)?

70. Do you have a qualified close friend or family member who is willing to provide you with low-cost legal services?

71. Do you have a strong business acumen, such that you feel comfortable managing the various aspects of your music career?

I know. It was a *very* long list of questions. Congratulations for making it all the way to the end without giving up on your music career and becoming a dentist instead. Answering each of those questions will serve you in filling out the "My Strengths" and "My Weaknesses" sheets. You might not have the time or energy to answer all of the questions, but try to get to as many as you can. After some brainstorming, your sheets should look something like Figure B. Figure B shows one of the sample sheets of a fictional artist.

Figure B

My Strengths

I own fairly decent music recording equipment and I know how to use it. I can make good recordings w/o a studio.

I am good at writing many songs quickly.

I have great relationships with a lot of other musicians in my area.

I know how to record and edit videos and I have good recording equipment.

I have a lot of fans who are into geek culture. My music and my personality is popular with this demographic.

I think my music would be well suited for use in science fiction movies, TV, and video games.

I have a very large presence on Twitter.

I know a lot about science and astronomy.

My Weaknesses

I have zero skill in graphic arts. I have no artwork for my recordings and I don't have a logo.

My website is not very engaging.

I am shy in front of crowds. I also get very nervous performing music in public.

I currently don't offer any kind of merchandise to my fans.

I don't have a lot of money.

I am not very good at writing long blog articles for my website.

I live in a small town that does not have a very engaging music scene.

I don't have any "industry" contacts, including contacts with PR companies, song pluggers, or publishing administrators.

I hope the above list of questions gave you a greater understanding of all of the moving parts in your entertainment operation. Hopefully, you now have a stronger appreciation for how many different skills and assets you'll need to be successful. Don't be alarmed if you found yourself answering "No" to the vast majority of these questions. The point of this exercise was not to determine whether or not you are good at a lot of things. In fact, most musicians tend to only excel in a few of the above areas.

The true purpose of this exercise was twofold: (1) to determine which things you *are* good at so you can make the most of those things, and (2) to determine (and to make you aware of) which things you are *not* so good at so that you can begin to minimize the potential harmful impact of those lapses in your network or skillset. The more aware you are of the answers to all of the above questions, the better your chances of having a successful entertainment career. The next step in the career plan process will show you how to optimize your potential for success.

Step 3: Maximizing Your Strengths and Minimizing Your Weaknesses

Now that you've inventoried your strengths and weaknesses, it's time to translate those attributes into specific career actions you can take. Doing this will help you make the most of your strengths and minimize the potential harm of your weaknesses.

Merely knowing your positive and negative characteristics will only take you so far. Forming a career plan also requires that you take each of those characteristics into account and devise tangible steps you can take to move your livelihood forward. To do this, you will first need to take your "My Strengths" and "My Weaknesses" sheets and label the top of the right-hand side of each sheet with the phrase "Action Plan." In this step of creating your career plan, you will consider each of your strengths and weaknesses and decide what specific career action you can take to move yourself forward. We will start with the "My Strengths" side and then move to the "My Weaknesses" side.

Your Strengths

Turn your attention to the "My Strengths" document you are preparing. At this point, the left side of each of your "Strengths" sheets should be filled with an array of positive characteristics that you can use to drive your career forward. Hopefully, answering the questions above revealed to you a lot of strengths of which you were not previously aware. Using the strengths you listed, you will now brainstorm specific, tangible actions that you will take to advance your music operation. You will list these actions on the "Action Plan" side of the document next to the corresponding "Strength" that inspired the "Action Plan."

At this point, you might be wondering "How do I come up with specific action plans for each of my strengths?" Well, this is where you will need to flex that creative, entrepreneurial mind of yours. Read the first strength on the page, and ask yourself "How can I use this ability to make my entertainment business more successful? How can I use this strength to my specific advantage?" Write down your action plan that results from that particular strength and repeat that process for every item on your "My Strengths" document.

Here are a few words of advice when it comes to writing effective action plans:

Be specific and don't skimp on the detail

The more specific and detailed your action plans are, the more you will get out of this exercise. For example, let's say that one of your strengths is your impressive ability to write great songs very quickly. If you write "I will write a ton of songs" as your action plan, that is hardly specific enough to show how you will use this (quite valuable) strength to advance your career. Your action plan should include specifics, and answer questions like: Why will you write those songs? What will you do with those songs once you write them? How will writing those songs specifically help your career?

For instance, consider the following as an action plan for this strength: "As a way to promote my career, I will write and record a new two-minute song every week for a year. I will record each song on a simple home setup to save money. I will release each of these songs on my YouTube channel, my personal website, and my social media pages. I will call this segment 'Two Minutes With [Your Name]'."

This revised action plan is better for two reasons. First, it provides specific details as to how you will use your prolific songwriting ability by presenting a clear, intriguing idea and including a precise temporal component. Second, the language also clearly demonstrates how this action plan will positively benefit your career. In this case, your two-minute recordings will not be sold for money. Instead, the songs will serve as a promotional vehicle to generate buzz for you as an artist.

Multiple action plans from one strength/Multiple strengths for one action plan

In many cases, a strength from your list may give rise to more than one action plan. For example, if one of your strengths is that you are good at producing your own recordings, you should be able to conjure more than one way to use that talent to move your career forward. If you are indeed a good producer, you can write in the right-hand column something like: "I will more efficiently create my own content for a full-length album by producing my own recordings rather than having to pay for a producer." Moreover, this skill could give rise to additional action plans, such as "I will raise my profile in the music industry and increase my income by producing music for other musicians in my local area."

Furthermore, you can create additional action plans by combining several of your strengths together. Some of your more ambitious (and possibly lucrative) projects as a music entrepreneur will require leveraging multiple areas of skill to achieve a particular goal. Making the most of your abilities means figuring out all of the ways your various gifts can be synergized to benefit your entertainment organization.

For example, let's say you are particularly good at cooking (Question 40). By itself, it would be hard to see how having culinary skill can advance your music career. But let's say you also happen to have good video recording equipment (Question 36), a strong Internet presence (Questions 27 and 33-35), and a decent catalogue of your own recorded music (Question 1). If you put all of these strengths together, then perhaps you could create a cooking webseries for your fans to watch. Each month, you could add a new episode showing your fans how to cook some of your favorite dishes. You could put the series on your website, streaming video sites, and your social media pages. Creating such a webseries would promote you as an entertainment personality and allow your fans to get to know you better. Moreover, you could put your recorded music into the webseries, which would expose your music to a wider audience.

Be creative

Finally, when creating action plans based on your strengths, it is critical to set your mind free and come up with creative ideas. Don't feel like your action plans have to follow the same path as the popular artists who have preceded you. Be bold. Take risks. The most successful independent musicians I have come across are the ones that have managed to use their strengths in imaginative ways. They have achieved their popularity by doing things differently, which allowed them to capture people's attention in an increasingly crowded music industry. There are artists out there who style their fans' hair after gigs, who crochet their band's logo onto earrings and then sell them online, who release an original music video every week for months at a time, who design their own costumes (which they wear on stage and then sell as merchandise), and who engage in many other equally original action plans. All of these are examples of artists who have identified their skills and have found unique ways to use them to advance their music operation. If you think hard enough, you can surely come up with some equally creative ideas of your own.

After you write down all of your action plans, the formatting of your "My Strengths" papers should resemble those of our fictional artist as depicted in Figure C below. If you were not able to come up with action plans for each of your strengths, don't worry. Reading the career advice in the remaining chapters of this book will likely provide you with additional ideas to fill in the vacant spots in your right-hand column. That being said, you should not feel required to leverage every single one of your strengths in furtherance of your career. It is likely not possible for you to connect every single one of your gifts into a tangible action plan.

Finally, be willing to revisit this column from time to time. Some of your best action plan ideas will likely pop into your head later, as you continue your work as an entertainer.

Figure C

My Strengths

I own fairly decent music recording equipment and I know how to use it. I can make good recordings w/o a studio.

I am good at writing many songs quickly.

I have great relationships with a lot of other musicians in my area.

I know how to record and edit videos and I have good recording equipment.

I have a lot of fans who are into geek culture. My music and my personality is popular with this demographic.

I think my music would be well suited for use in science fiction movies, TV, and video games.

I have a very large presence on Twitter.

I know a lot about science and astronomy.

To promote my music, I will write and record one new professionally-produced song every month and send it out to my fans on my social media pages, on YouTube, and on SoundCloud. Periodically, the song that I release will be recorded with a full band, which I will recruit by trading favors with other musicians in my area that I know.

To promote my music, I will use my prolific music and video creation skills to turn many, if not all, of my recordings into music videos. I will use my strong Twitter following to heavily promote each video I create, turning each video into a major promotional event. Moreover, I will also release videos showing the "making of" process for each music video. The more video content I can create, the better.

To begin creating a significant income stream, I will begin to market my music toward getting placements in science fiction movies, TV, and video games. I will start making contacts to the relevant people in these fields to slowly make these opportunities available to me. I will start attending more pop culture conventions to meet some independent content developers in these forms of media. That would be a good way for me to start. I will also start reaching out to, and networking with, song pluggers.

I will post frequently about science and astronomy subjects on Twitter to strengthen my brand.

To further promote my brand, engage with my audience, and cater to my unique talents, I will create and host a YouTube show where I will talk about science and astronomy in an interesting and engaging way. I will feature my own music on my show and direct viewers to purchase my music through the videos. I will promote the show to my massive Twitter following and market it to my geek-culture fans. I will make appearances at science and pop culture conventions to further establish my brand in this area. Eventually, I can even write books on these subjects.

Your Weaknesses

When it comes to creating action plans, it is not enough to just figure out how to capitalize on your strengths. It is equally important to develop concrete strategies to prevent your weaknesses from dragging you down.

No artist has a flawless music operation. Even the truly exceptional will have many imperfections in their organization. Going through the above questions likely revealed your various weak spots. Maybe you don't have a lot of money in your bank account. Maybe you have not written very many songs yet. Maybe you don't have easy access to recording equipment. Maybe you aren't very good with social media. Whatever your weaknesses are, you need to develop action plans to address each one. To do this, you will need to take your "My Weaknesses" sheets and write down an action plan in the right-hand column for each of your corresponding weaknesses. Basically, what you just did with your "My Strengths" sheets, you will now do with your "My Weaknesses" sheets.

You may not feel particularly excited at the prospect of having to address all of your deficiencies. It is, understandably, much more fun to make plans for the things you do well than to stew in the things you do poorly. However, you will be pleased to know that the process for developing action plans for your shortcomings is a relatively simple process. This is because, when you are faced with a weakness, there are basically only three actions you can take. You can either:

1. Overcome the weakness,
2. outsource the weakness, or
3. avoid the weakness.

Since those are the only things you can do with a particular flaw in your operation, all of the action plans in your "My Weaknesses" document will involve doing one of those three things in a particular way.

Action plan: overcome the weakness

The first type of action plan to address a weakness is perhaps the most obvious: simply overcome it. Work hard to make your weakness no longer a weakness. Many flaws can be eliminated with a little study and/or effort. The best approach for dealing with these gaps in your abilities is to work at them until you improve those skills. Use the "overcome it" approach for weaknesses that are (1) particularly critical to your vision of a successful career and (2) within your ability to overcome with hard work.

Many musicians, for example, are uncomfortable performing in front of live audiences. In fact, even some music legends (including Cher, Adele, Barbra Streisand, and David Bowie) have suffered from bouts of stage fright. But despite its prevalence, this particular weakness can be quite harmful for artists. Today's performers tend to make the lion's share of their income from live performances. Thus, anything that might impede you from regularly and effectively playing gigs presents a significant threat to your career's viability. So, if stage fright is one of your weaknesses (Question 45), it is in your interest to brainstorm action plans to try to personally overcome this problem. A quick Google search can provide you with a number of actions you can take to help beat the butterflies. These include things like breathing exercises, seeking therapy, or performing in front of smaller crowds and working up to bigger ones.

Just because you are not good at something now does not mean you have to stay that way forever. To achieve your goals in the music industry, it is important for you to find the deficiencies that are within your ability to personally fix, and then fix them. Overcoming these obstacles will be the principal way that you grow as an artist and an entrepreneur. Other than by searching the Internet, reading books, and picking the brains of other music professionals, one important way that you will learn to overcome many of your weaknesses will be by absorbing the career advice contained within this book. So read on!

Action plan: outsource the weakness

In some cases, you will come across a weakness of yours that is critical for you to conquer but, no matter how hard you try, you may not be able to personally overcome that weakness with hard work. In those cases, you should recall musician Kim Boekbinder's advice from the previous chapter: "Know your strengths. Do those things. Know your weaknesses. Don't do those things." If you have a flaw that you cannot fix but you need fixed, then get someone else to fix it.

For a handful of your weaknesses, the best action plan may involve delegating that weakness to others. For example, you will frequently encounter legal issues as a musician-entrepreneur. There will be contracts to review, intellectual property issues to handle, and (though hopefully not too frequently) lawsuits to defend. Legal issues are an inevitable byproduct of a thriving music career, so if you do not have easy and low-cost access to a lawyer (Question 70), then this would most certainly constitute a weakness for you.

Is a lack of legal services the sort of weakness that you can personally overcome? Not unless you are willing to take three years off from your career to attend law school. Granted, with a little study, you can probably learn to do some basic, legal-ish tasks (like registering your song copyrights). But for most of your important legal work, outsourcing will be your only option to handle this weakness. Therefore, an appropriate action plan here would involve taking measures to seek out effective legal representation without busting your budget. This might mean getting a referral from a fellow music professional or receiving pro bono help from a VLA (Volunteer Lawyers for the Arts) organization in your area.

Action plan: avoid the weakness

Finally, you might address some of your weaknesses by avoiding them entirely. In some cases, it may not be in your interest to try to overcome a deficiency or delegate it to others. Instead, you may decide just to de-emphasize that area in your music operation, thus preventing that weakness from hurting your career.

"Avoidance" action plans are best for weaknesses that are not critical for you to conquer to be successful. For a few of your weaknesses, you may decide "I just won't do that particular thing very often." Obviously, you can't take this approach with many of your career activities. If stage fright is one of your weaknesses, deciding not to do live performances is likely out of the question for most artists. If you don't have any lawyers in your inner circle, it would be disastrous for you to eschew getting legal services entirely. Some weaknesses you just can't avoid.

But some weaknesses may only address what would be a minor aspect of many musicians' careers. These weaknesses are prime candidates for avoidance-based action plans. For example, you may not be particularly good at personally making any sort of unique item that you could sell to your fans (like clothing or original artwork, Question 66). Theoretically, you could address this weakness by *learning* how to make some kind of item (an "overcome the weakness" action plan) or delegating the making of these items to a third party (an "outsource the weakness" action plan). But in this situation, you could elect not to expend any of your resources on selling unique items of merchandise. You may decide, in your managerial judgment, that your music career will not live or die on your ability to peddle handmade tchotchkes. In such a case, simply avoiding the weakness may be the best action plan.

Once you have a good handle on the three types of action plans, filling in your "My Weaknesses" sheets becomes quite manageable. You will devise an action plan on the right-hand side of the document for each of your weaknesses. Each action plan will be based on one of the three action plan types. For each weakness, you will decide whether to:

- Overcome the weakness (for important weaknesses which you are capable of personally defeating),
- outsource the weakness (for important weaknesses which are more difficult for you to personally defeat), or
- avoid the weakness (for unimportant weaknesses that you need not defeat to have a successful career).

Once you decide how you will approach the weakness generally, you will devise a specific plan to overcome, outsource, or avoid it. Figure D shows an example of our fictional artist devising action plans for some of her weaknesses.

Figure D

My Weaknesses

I have zero skill in graphic arts. I have no artwork for my recordings and I don't have a logo.

OUTSOURCE: Since I probably can't teach myself to draw, but I will use websites like fiverr.com to find people who can design logos and album artwork for me at low cost.

My website is not very engaging.

OVERCOME: I will revamp my website using a sharp-looking Wordpress shell. I will watch some YouTube videos and read some books on web design to learn how to make engaging site content.

I am shy in front of crowds. I also get very nervous performing music in public.

OVERCOME: Live performing is too important for me to simply avoid it. I will study some materials on how to conquer stage fright and I will start by playing small gigs to build my confidence. I will also join a group like Toastmasters to slowly become more comfortable around others.

I currently don't offer any kind of merchandise to my fans.

OVERCOME: I will use websites like Cafepress to create personalized T-shirts with a newly-created logo on them. I will also look into creating astronomy-themed merchandise for my science-related music content.

I don't have a lot of money.

OVERCOME: I will conquer my stage fright and play more paying gigs. Moreover, I will pursue sales and licensing opportunities for my music and slowly work toward monetizing my YouTube videos. I will also heavily crowdfund my projects.

I am not very good at writing long blog articles for my website.

AVOID: I do not need to write lengthy blogs to reach my audience. Short tweets and engaging video can be my primary means of communication.

I live in a small town that does not have a very engaging music scene.

OVERCOME: I have done a pretty good job of getting a good social media following for myself despite living in a small town. However, eventually, I will need to save enough resources to move to a better city for my career. I will begin planning a budget for that now.

I don't have any "industry" contacts, including contacts with PR companies, song pluggers, or publishing administrators.

OVERCOME: I will dedicate myself to networking more each day. Moreover, I will specifically set aside one day each week that I will dedicate entirely to networking with industry professionals. I will reach out to them via e-mail Twitter, either directly or (whenever possible) by getting an introduction through someone I already know.

Step 4: Set Your Organization's Goals

At this point in the career plan process, you have (1) determined whether you are ready for a career as an artist-entrepreneur, (2) taken inventory of your strengths and weaknesses, and (3) developed action plans based on those strengths and weaknesses. Now comes the final step: setting your organization's goals (your career goals).

As with any business organization, having clear goals will give your entertainment operation a vital sense of direction and purpose. It is critical for you to firmly establish the things you wish to accomplish as an artist-entrepreneur, both in the short-term and long-term. By doing so, you will keep yourself motivated and ensure that all of your career decisions are made with your overarching objectives in mind.

To set the goals for your entertainment organization, you first need to ask yourself what you want your future to look like. Take out a new sheet of paper (as if you haven't massacred enough trees already) and answer these three questions:

1) Short Term: What do you want your entertainment organization and career to look like in one year?
2) Medium Term: What do you want your entertainment organization and career to look like in five years?
3) Long Term: What do you want your entertainment organization and career to look like in ten to twenty years?

Be as detailed as possible when answering these questions. Close your eyes and envision what you want your organization to look like one, five, and ten years from now: How many songs have you written? How many recordings do you have? Through what methods are people listening to your recordings? What does your social media presence look like? Do you have employees or service providers? What do they do for you? How often and where are you performing? How are your finances? Are you able to completely support yourself with just your music? How are you perceived by the public? Are you involved with any other entertainment or business activities outside of your music?

Based on your descriptions, your career in the long-term should look more impressive than your career in the medium-term, which should in turn look more impressive than your short-term outlook. Be sure that your short-, medium-, and long-term goals are ambitious, yet reasonable. If you predicted that you would still be working a non-music day job to support your art ten years from now, you are not aiming high enough. Conversely, if you envisioned going from zero to platinum-selling multimillionaire in just twelve short months, then you need to be a *lot* more realistic.

The format of your paper should look something like Figure E.

Figure E

Short-term Goal

I will have written and recorded a new album's worth of recorded material. This material will consist of professionally-produced recordings that I can send out to my fans. Many of these songs will be recorded with a full band and/or made into music videos. I will distribute those songs out to a wide audience. I will have an appreciably larger social media following and I will start to have somewhat of a YouTube presence. I will continue working at my day job to help fund my music career, but I will also start finding some ways to monetize my content.

Medium-term Goal

I will have written and recorded five album's worth of recorded material, all professional quality. I will distribute these songs out to a wide audience, which will be in the 6-7 figures on Twitter. I will be a popular YouTube personality with a successful show about science and astronomy that features my original music. I will be recognized as a scientific authority in the pop culture community and get invited to speak at conferences and other events. I will have science-related merchandise to sell to my fans. I will also have some of my songs featured in movies, television, and video games. I will also start doing live performances at a somewhat steady clip.

Long-term Goal

I will be a household name. I will have well over 100 professionally-produced songs that I have written and will have recorded and released over 40 music videos. My YouTube show about science and astronomy will be among the most popular shows in the genre, and I will receive opportunities to create a version of my show for cable television. I will also perform frequently, touring the world on a regular basis. My show will feature me performing my catalogue of songs and discussing scientific concepts. This show will be popular at traditional performance venues and also at colleges, academic conferences, and sci-fi conventions. I will have written at least two books about science. My music will be featured frequently in movies, television, and video games. In fact, I will have been hired multiple times by production companies to compose the entire musical score for several movie, TV, and video game projects.

Once you craft your three main goals, flip your paper over, and divide that side into three sections. Label them "1-year," "5-year," and "10-20 years." Within each of your three sections, you will write down the specific things you will do to reach your short-term, medium-term, and long-term career goals. You will write down the steps you will need to take to reach your 1-year, 5-year, and 10-20-year benchmarks. To make this exercise even more useful for you, I strongly recommend that you come up with an estimated date for when you intend to complete each step. This is a particularly useful thing to do with your 1-year entries, since you will be working on these tasks right away.

You might be asking, "How do I come up with the steps I need to take to reach these goals?" Well, I have some good news for you: You already did! Assuming that you completed Step 3 of the career plan process with a high level of detail, then you already should have a long list of action plans to advance every facet of your career as an artist-entrepreneur. Now all you need to do is take the action plans you wrote and incorporate them into your short-, medium-, and long-term goals. In other words, you will arrange your action plans on the sheet in such a way that they will cause you to achieve your three goals. In Figure F, you will see how our fictional artist arranged her action plans into steps to achieve her goals. Note how our fictional artist broke some of her action plans up into smaller steps that would help her reach her goals in all three time periods.

Figure F

1 year (M = Month)

- **Every Month (throughout career):** Write/record one new-professionally-produced song each month. Distribute each song to my large Twitter following. Begin researching ways to monetize this content.

- **M 3, 6, 9, 12:** Use my band contacts to have that month's song be recorded with a full band (trade favors with other musicians). Make this song into a music video using my video tools and post them on a YouTube channel. Post "making of" videos to YouTube as well to create more content.

- **M5:** Begin seeking help to cure stage fright. Join Toastmasters; attend meetings regularly.

- **YouTube show:** M1: Begin planning process for creating my science/astronomy show on YouTube. Find someone on Fiverr to create a logo and artwork for the show. M3: Begin researching astronomy subjects more significantly to become more able to discuss these topics. M6: Launch first episode of my YouTube show. I will initially do two episodes per month. By beginning of next year, make it a weekly show and begin researching ways to monetize the content (sponsorships, YouTube ads, etc.)

5 years (Y = Year)

- **Y2:** Begin setting aside one day each week to network, looking both for (i) conferences where I can be a guest speaker about science/astronomy and (ii) song pluggers who can get my music content in media. Begin aggressively promoting my Twitter handle wherever I go to increase my social media following. Move through the ranks at Toastmasters to become 100% comfortable in front of groups. Begin using crowdfunding campaigns to ensure sufficient resources for current/future projects.

- **Y3:** Focus heavily on building the YouTube show. Look for licensing opportunities with song pluggers. But I will not wait for pluggers to find opportunities for me; I will actively seek opportunities myself through my networking contacts. Build relationships with music supervisors at various media companies, and even volunteer to place my music in small movie, TV, and game projects to build my credentials. Begin researching science-themed merchandising options for my music.

- **Y4:** Create a 2-hour music and science live show that will feature my own music and discussion of science and astronomy concepts. It will be like a live, expanded version of my weekly YouTube show. Seek opportunities to present this show at conferences and colleges. Be willing to present the show at a low price to build audience for it. Expand my music licensing endeavors further. Expand crowdfunding efforts.

137

❖ **–Y5:** Have full array of science merchandise to offer to fans online and at my live shows. Expand promotion of YouTube show, live shows, and music by retaining the services of publicists as needed.

10-20 Years (Y = Year)

❖ **Phase 1 (Y5-Y8):** Invest heavily in publicists as funds permit to promote YouTube show, live performances, and music. Use massive Twitter following (now well into the 7 figures) to further assist in this regard. Network heavily to further increase media placement opportunities for my content. Reach out to booking agents to start getting more dates for my music & science live show. Begin writing and self-publishing first science book.

❖ **Phase 2: (Y9-Y12):** Live show is nationwide. Create DVD of live show to sell online. Continue to aggressively pursue media placements and start using my contacts to get opportunities to compose musical scores for movies, TV, and video games. Write second book.

❖ **Phase 3 (Y12+):** Continue aggressive push of my various revenue streams, continuing to invest the significant resources that I have accumulated.

Once you have filled out this sheet of paper, you now have your comprehensive career plan. Congratulations! You have identified your strengths and weaknesses, converted those strengths and weaknesses into action plans, and incorporated those action plans into concrete steps to achieve your short-term, medium-term, and long-term career goals.

Your career will be a difficult journey, but your goals document will be the map that guides you along the way. Before you make any decision for your entertainment organization, check this document to make sure it fits within the goals you wish to accomplish. With your career plan firmly in place, you are well positioned to make effective decisions for yourself, your art, and your business.

The Only Constant is Change

One last note: Never forget that your career plan documents are *living* documents. You will need to constantly revisit all of them as your career moves forward and your organization grows and changes. You will be updating them frequently. Be sure to set aside time every year to make the necessary changes to your career plan. As you develop as an artist and a businessperson, you will attain new strengths and endure new weaknesses. As a result of these changes, you will need to revise your action plans and even create some new ones. Moreover, with each new year, you will need a new one-year short-term goal. And as you achieve a particular career goal, you will need to make a new one to take its place. Dedication to constant improvement is the hallmark of a successful artist-entrepreneur.

PART III

THE SECTORS OF YOUR INDEPENDENT MUSIC EMPIRE

CHAPTER 11

YOUR CONTENT CREATION, DISTRIBUTION, AND PUBLISHING

The ABCs of Content

Repeat after me: Your content is king.

Your content isn't just important for your career—your content *is* your career. Your ability to create lots of content and distribute it effectively will drive every other aspect of your entertainment organization. Without a strong content sector, every other area suffers. Your organization might be great at promotion, but that is irrelevant if it has nothing to promote. You could be a spectacular live performer, but you will only get so far by performing other artists' material at your gigs.

With every piece of original content you create—whether it is an original song, recording, video, or even a podcast, webseries, poem, painting, novel, or anything else your creative mind can conjure—your organization gains one additional revenue-generating copyright. Each of those copyrights provides you with countless opportunities to license, sell copies of, perform, and make derivative works of your creations. Taking advantage of these opportunities can advance your art, raise your profile, and make you rich.

Given the role that creating original content plays in driving your career, you need to be prolific when it comes to generating new material. A lot of early-career musicians fall into the trap of creating only a handful of original songs and then riding those songs for years without creating anything new. Your fans' appetite for new content is insatiable. They will only listen to the same stuff over and over for so long before they move on to another artist. Nothing is more annoying for music fans than going to watch a local artist perform multiple times in a year and enduring the same set list each time.

So, with apologies to Alec Baldwin's character in *Glengarry Glen Ross*, I wish to co-opt the famous sales maxim "ABC: Always Be Closing." I wish to provide for you a new "ABC" principle that you need to follow as an artist-entrepreneur: Always Be Creating.

Create all the time. Never stop generating and distributing quality content. Will this require a lot of work on your part?

Absolutely. But you can do it, and you *have* to do it to succeed. Your fans will never complain about getting too much content, but having too little content will run your organization straight into the ground. This chapter will go over the basics of creating and distributing content for your music organization. And as you absorb these lessons, be sure to practice them within the context of our ABC principle. In the new music industry, content creation and distribution will be a constant, year-round endeavor for you. This chapter will provide you with insight on how to operate in this area effectively.

Out with the Old; In with the New.

The Old

Achieving success with your content as an artist-entrepreneur will require that you abandon the conventional ways that artists produce and distribute their material. Instead, you need to take advantage of 21st century technology and embrace the digital revolution to get the most out of your creations. The music industry is undergoing a paradigm shift when it comes to content. Luckily for you, this shift greatly favors independent artists, and serves to wither the competitive advantage that record labels have historically enjoyed in the production and sale of recorded music.

You are no doubt quite aware of the prevailing content creation and distribution model for most established recording artists. Every eighteen months or so, your favorite musician releases about a dozen recordings all at once in the form of an LP (Long Play) album. These songs were written and recorded over the course of several months (or more) using some very expensive equipment. No doubt the project involved a top-of-the-line recording studio, or several studios, and a small army of producers, engineers, mixers, and other folks. Each song cost a big pile of money to make, which you then have to multiply by the number of total songs on the album.

And, as if this endeavor was not expensive enough already, money also has to be spent to promote and distribute the album. The hefty promo budget will likely include one or two high-priced music videos, which often fail to help move product because "expensive" does not necessarily mean "engaging." And distribution

144

will not come cheap either. The labor, transportation, and infrastructure required to get physical CDs throughout the world will eat a big chunk out of any potential profits.

In short, creating music and getting it out there under the conventional model requires a small fortune. Oh, and in case you forgot: Given the way that most record contracts are structured, the artist is ultimately bearing much of these costs through label recoupment (See Chapter 3). In short, these expenses are unnecessarily high, and it is ultimately the artist who will be on the receiving end of this financial butt-kicking.

The New

The conventional content creation and distribution method is bad news for artists, and it is a particularly unsustainable model for the independent artist-entrepreneur in the early stages of their career. If you are just starting out, you likely have neither the money nor the time nor the resources to do things this way. It would be insane for anyone in your situation to try to record twelve songs in a top-shelf studio, film a couple high-priced videos, and execute an expensive distribution campaign all within a short time period. And then, once you complete that herculean effort, it would be equally insane for you to sit around not releasing anything new for eighteen months while the listening public forgets that you exist.

Most of the artists you know and love might do things this way, but it is the wrong approach for an emerging artist-entrepreneur—especially one with access to today's technology. Recording and releasing a bunch of content within a short time window made more sense in an era where recording and releasing content was an unavoidably expensive proposition. In an era where creation and distribution involved expensive recording equipment and high-priced physical distribution, bunching one's content together to keep costs down was the best possible option. But today, there is a better way for indie artists. This chapter will show you how to use this new technological landscape to effectively, efficiently, and *inexpensively* create and distribute your content.

145

Making Your Recorded Music

Early Stages of Your Career

When you are in the fledgling stages of building your music empire, you most likely will not have access to the high-priced studios and equipment that popular artists traditionally use to record their songs. Studio time, labor, hardware, software—these things cost a bundle. These dandy little amenities are out of the reach of most early-career indies. Granted, I'm not making a blanket statement for all artists here. Maybe you do have access to these resources for some reason: Maybe your friend owns a studio, your uncle is a recording engineer, or maybe you're just a gazillionaire. If you are one of these lucky folks, then bully for you! That will give you a nice head start as you get your career off the ground. Go record in your top-shelf studio and bang out some tunes, oh charmed one.

But for the rest of you mere mortals who have yet to sip from that particular golden chalice, you will need to make do with more affordable equipment. Luckily, as you learned back in Chapter 8, it is now possible for artists to build a decent home studio with only a small up-front investment. And with the emergence of free and nearly-free DAW software and plenty of ways to easily learn how to use it, you can make good-quality music without leaving your home or lightening your wallet.

You may have some concerns about producing your early-career recordings in a simple home studio: "Won't the quality be worse than if I used a professional studio?" "Won't I need other singers and musicians to create my recordings? What if I can't afford to hire those people?" "What about mixing and mastering my recordings?" It is understandable that you have these worries. When you listen to some of your favorite recording artists, you hear music that is expertly-produced by highly-qualified professionals. No doubt you can also hear a large number of musicians on that record. "How can I possibly create something so grandiose by myself at home?" you might ask.

Here's the thing about that: In this stage of your career, you don't *have* to. As an up-and-coming artist-entrepreneur, your music is serving a different purpose than that of an established artist. As a result, your early-career recordings don't need the same bells and whistles. Those artists are trying to sell millions of records. That requires top-quality, heavily-produced material. That is not what you are trying to do with your music.

"Hold on," I can hear you saying. "That is *exactly* what I am trying to do with my music. What the hell do you mean I'm not trying to sell millions of records? Of course I am trying to sell millions of records. That's the whole point!" Fair enough. Selling a ton of your music is certainly a good long-term goal to have. But that is not your immediate goal for your early-career material (if it is, you need to revisit your career plan).

When starting out as an independent artist-entrepreneur, your early recordings serve a different function. This music is meant to *promote* you and your entertainment organization, not be sold in mass quantities. You won't make very much money from selling your music initially anyway, seeing as you won't have much name recognition when you are starting out. Instead, your goal should be to make your music as widely available as possible to raise your profile and build your fan base. To do this, you will need to get your music in front of as many ears as possible. This means allowing people to listen to your early-career material *for free* on the Internet.

That's right. You will be *giving away* this music online so that people can find out about you. So the bad news is that you won't get rich selling your recordings early on. But the good news is that these promotional records don't need to be made in a professional studio. As long as your material is engaging, a simple home setup is good enough to create recordings that get you the Facebook shares and YouTube views you need to reach the next level.

Think about some of your favorite Internet artists who have had songs go viral in recent years. Many of those songs were recorded on the sort of hardware and software that anyone can get at any consumer electronics store. And once you get that basic equipment, you already have the requisite tools to start your career as a recording artist.

Later Stages of Your Career

As your career starts to grow, your recording procedures will evolve accordingly. Once you have enough fans that selling your music might make financial sense, you may decide that you want to record in a better studio. You can do this by either (1) upgrading the equipment in your home studio or (2) renting out time in a professional studio in your area. Both approaches have their benefits. Option 1 gives you more control over your future recording projects and, once you pay for it, the equipment is yours forever and you won't have to pay to rent out studio time. Option 2 allows you to avoid equipment ownership costs and saves you the trouble of having to learn how to use any new toys. You will need to review your situation as an artist and determine which approach is best for you and your career. Both of these recording methods are going to be a little pricier than your home studio. If you do not have the money for these items when you need them, you might want to review some of the fundraising tips outlined in Chapter 14.

As your recording projects become more ambitious, you will also need a larger cast of characters to bring them to fruition. Much of your early work might only need a single performer—you. You and your guitar, you and your piano, or maybe you recording yourself playing multiple instruments on different tracks that you then mix together (if you are particularly skilled). Eventually, though, as your recordings get more elaborate, you will need some help. You might need people to play other instruments, or perhaps provide additional vocals.

If you are already in a band, then obviously this is not a problem for you. But if you are a solo artist, you will need to go out and find this extra labor. This is why networking is so important. Becoming well-acquainted with other musicians in your area (perhaps by joining a local musicians' cooperative) will help you find people who are willing to perform on your records—particularly if you similarly agree to lend your services for their works.

You will also need more than a few extra musicians to make this music. More complicated recordings require the contributions of other professionals. If you record in an actual studio, you will need an engineer to help put your recordings together. If you intend for your music to achieve the highest possible quality, you should also have your tracks professionally mastered. A good mastering house will fix minor flaws in your recordings and equalize your audio within and across each song. And if you want your recording to be *truly* impressive, and you have the funds for it, getting a producer to help you make your record would be a particularly wise idea. A music producer serves a similar function that a film director does for a movie. They control all aspects of the recording process and can help make your recordings reach their full potential.

The best way to find these resources is through networking. Getting referrals from musicians and other music professionals in your area will increase the possibility of finding someone who has experience with your style of music and who can work within your budget. Failing that, there are various Internet resources you can use to find the people you need. Websites like Craigslist, LinkedIn, SessionPlayers, and SoundBetter can be very helpful in this regard.

All of this extra help has to be compensated, unfortunately. If you rent out a studio, you might get lucky and the facility will throw in an engineer as part of your rental fee. Otherwise, these folks can usually be compensated on a flat fee or hourly basis. Mastering houses tend to be paid by the song.

Where things can get a little tricky is with producers. Producing a recording project can be a significant undertaking, particularly when the producer is working on several tracks for you. Some producers will work on a flat fee, a per-song fee, or a per-hour arrangement. Their asking prices can be quite high, however. In some situations, a producer might be willing to reduce or even eliminate an up-front charge in exchange for back-end royalties on each record you sell. These arrangements are more complicated to put together than a simple flat payment. Thus, you should consult an attorney before signing any sort of agreement of that nature.

But when deciding how to compensate anyone who works on your recordings, be sure to heed the advice from Chapter 9. Almost any method of paying the people in your empire is acceptable, except for selling your copyrights. *Never* sell any part of your copyrights to get the recording services you need. This situation will most likely present itself with producers. Someone may express a willingness to produce your record in exchange for part copyright ownership in the recording created. Be sure to never, ever do this. As we previously discussed, your copyrights are the soul of your music operation, and they are too damn valuable to sell to get any services you need. You can pay your producers a flat fee, you can pay them by the hour, or you can even give them royalties. But your copyrights are not for sale.

Timing Your Music Releases

Early Stages of Your Career

As discussed earlier in the chapter, most of your favorite artists release their new music in bunches. Every year or two (assuming no delays, which there often are), big-name performers will unload about a dozen recordings on you all at the same time in the form of an album of music. The artist and label will then hope that the album is memorable enough that the artist will continue to remain within the public's consciousness during the period between albums.

As an up-and-coming independent artist-entrepreneur, releasing your music in a similar fashion would be a colossally bad idea. First of all, when you are starting out, you likely won't have the necessary resources to create a bunch of quality recordings at the same time. Your funds are quite limited, and you have to spend your money wisely in the early-going.

Second, releasing a bunch of songs every couple years does not support the goals your early music needs to achieve for you. If your goal is to sell your music for money, releasing full albums might make more sense. Getting consumers to try to buy twelve tracks at the same time could mean more revenues. I say *could* because people are not buying full albums as much as they did a couple decades ago. But at least that is the rationale.

Nonetheless, remember that the goal for your early music is not its sale; it is to promote you as an artist. If you want your music to raise your profile, it does not make sense to have long periods of time in between releases of recordings. Thus, you should avoid releasing material in full albums. Instead, you should spread out releases so that you always have new material coming out. Instead of putting out a bunch of material all at once, release one or two items at a time every few weeks. Let each individual release be its own independent promotional event so that your audience never has a chance to forget about you. Trickling out your new content will constantly give your listeners a reason to pay attention to you. For

150

example, instead of releasing a twelve-song album, you are much better off releasing a new song every month for a year.

In the early stages of your career, you may find it difficult to create and record enough new material to even release something every few weeks. When you are starting out, and your time and resources are limited, it is hard to create significant amounts of new content. Despite these impediments, you should try as hard as you can to adhere to the ABC principle discussed in this chapter. No matter how tough it is to do so, Always Be Creating new content. Success tends to favor the prolific content creators. Fans can get bored of your old stuff pretty quickly.

But if you are struggling to get new material out there, there are some shortcuts you can take to keep a fresh stream of content flowing. In their book *The Indie Band Survival Guide*, Chertkow and Feehan recommend creating alternative versions of some of your previous songs as a way to maximize your releases. For example, you can take one of your old songs and create an acoustic version, a live version, an a cappella version, a remix, a version in a different genre, or a version in which you perform your song with another artist. Releasing new varieties of your old material is a great way to ensure that your fans are always getting more content. Try not to overly rely on this approach, however. Eventually, your fans will grow tired of constant adaptations and will want to see some genuinely new material from you.

Later Stages of Your Career

When you get to the point in your career where selling your music becomes a viable option, you may decide to alter your content release strategy. Once you have achieved a certain amount of fame, you could release your content as full albums every couple years the way many artists do. That being said, you may very well decide to continue spreading out your releases one at a time. Today's music consumers are shying away from buying full albums anyway. More and more, they favor buying only the individual songs they like and ignoring the rest of the songs on an album.

Therefore, as people increasingly decide to buy recordings one at a time, you may very well decide you are better off similarly releasing songs one at a time. Don't be afraid to try different approaches when it comes to the timing of your music releases. Maybe your fans will prefer getting singles from you. Maybe they will favor twelve-track albums. Or maybe they will respond most favorably to a happy medium in the form of three- to five-track EP (Extended Play) releases from you. Experiment with the different methods and choose whichever one maximizes your impact. But don't feel like you have to release full albums just because other artists do. Besides, that method may very well be on its way out as the music industry continues to evolve.

Distributing Your Music

Early Stages of Your Career

After you finish any new music content, you need to figure out how to get it to your listeners' ears. Now you are entering the exciting, and often complicated, world of music distribution.

There is certainly no shortage of ways to distribute your material. If you follow the example of the more famous artists out there, you may think that music distribution means finding a way to sell physical copies of your music in stores. Those stores could be in actual buildings, like Wal-Mart or Best Buy, or in virtual stores like Amazon.com or BandCamp.com. You can also sell digital copies of your music using a service like iTunes. But don't limit yourself. Today, distributing music often means going beyond the mere sale of physical or downloadable copies, and moving into streaming as well. Making your material available for streaming services like Pandora and Spotify is standard practice for prominent artists nowadays.

Will you be using these distribution methods when you are starting out? Perhaps, to some extent, you may. You will learn more about how to distribute your music these ways in the "Later Stages of Your Career" part of this section. But to understand the best way for an early-career artist to get their music out there, you must again remember the purpose your early career music serves: to promote you. And if promotion is the name of the game, you need a distribution method that will give your music worldwide reach cheaply and quickly. Luckily, such a distribution method exists—and it is called YouTube. For an up-and-coming artist-entrepreneur trying to promote their material, YouTube is a godsend.

Some of you might find this puzzling. You may be questioning why a website featuring videos of skateboarders eating pavement should be your music distribution platform. Well, one could make a pretty good argument that this repository for idiot skater footage may also be the best thing that has ever happened to indie musicians. Not that long ago, the costs required to get your music in front of a potential audience of over one billion people would be incalculable. Now, thanks to YouTube, it is absolutely *free*. Putting your recordings on YouTube—either as a music video, a live performance video, a lyric video, or otherwise—is ridiculously easy. You can create a "channel" for your videos in just minutes and start distributing your material right away.

For the above reasons, Eric Sussman (Amanda Palmer's manager) calls YouTube "one of the single greatest music innovations of the recent Internet age." He also notes how "people do not realize that YouTube is the #1 music streaming service in the world. Considering how large video files can be, for artists to have a one-stop place to post free video is kind of amazing. I don't think many folks could have imagined back in the early 2000s that YouTube would go on to become an incredible tool for artists."

Be thankful that you have this powerful service at your disposal. YouTube will be your music operation's primary distribution mechanism when you start out. That is how you will get much of your material within the reach of your current and future fans. In fact, you will still use YouTube a lot even when your career evolves and you begin to distribute your music through more conventional means. No matter the stage of your career, you will be well-served by using the site to post things like live concert footage, music videos, and random pieces of video content to keep your fans' interest piqued. The next chapter will tell you more about creating content on sites like YouTube.

Later Stages of Your Career

As your popularity grows, it will become more prudent for you to use the wide variety of content distribution methods available to you. Here is a collection of some of the many ways you can get your music out there:

153

Artist microsites (e.g., Bandcamp)

Bandcamp is an online platform in which artists create "microsite" pages for their music on the bandcamp.com site. On their microsite, the artist can offer their music for free streaming, sell their music for download, or sell physical copies of their music or other merchandise. Bandcamp allows artists to use "variable pricing" for the products the artist sells, meaning that the artist can choose to sell their music for as much or as little as they want on the site. The site even includes a feature to let the consumer "pay what they want" for the recording—a music sales technique popularized by artists such as Radiohead and Amanda Palmer. Artists can sign up for Bandcamp's basic service for free. The site makes its money by taking a 15% revenue share from the artist's digital sales (which can be reduced to 10% if the artist meets certain sales thresholds) and a 10% revenue share from all physical sales.

Online distribution services (e.g., TuneCore, CD Baby)

Eventually, your entertainment operation will evolve to the point where you will want to sell your music on more than just your own microsite. Online Distribution Services provide musicians with an easy, cheap, and efficient way to get their recorded material on digital platforms like iTunes and Amazon. They can even get your music set up on streaming services like Spotify. You can sign up with a few mouse clicks and the interfaces are generally user-friendly. Many of these providers also provide additional services as well, such as brick-and-mortar CD distribution, YouTube monetization, SoundExchange royalty collection (for when your recordings are played on Internet radio), and mechanical license procurement (if you want to sell your cover version of someone else's song), and even some limited music publishing and licensing services.

Each of these companies employs slightly different pricing models. For example, the popular distributor CD Baby charges a one-time fee for each album of yours it distributes and a 9% commission for each album sold. In contrast, the TuneCore service charges an annual fee for each of your albums it distributes. These fees total higher than the one-time CD Baby fee, but TuneCore does not charge a commission for each album it sells. As an artist-entrepreneur, you will need to make your own decisions about which pricing model works best for your particular situation. If you are just dipping your toe into online retailing, then something with a lower up-front cost might work better for you. If you anticipate more robust digital sales, then you might be more willing to pay annual fees to avoid per-sale commissions.

Full-service distributors

With hard work and good content, you can have a very successful distribution operation using nothing more than microsites and online distribution services. Musicians can make a lot of money and have great careers with these uncomplicated and inexpensive platforms. However, some artist-entrepreneurs who hit certain sales and fame levels might be well served by upgrading from an online service to a full-fledged distribution company. Full-service distributors can be independent companies or can even be affiliated with major record labels (such as Alternative Distribution Alliance or RED Distribution). These distributors will put some serious muscle behind your content. They do all of the same distribution activities as an online service but with more effectiveness and reach. These companies can also provide marketing and publicity services for your content and the largest distributors will even provide radio promotion.

Are there any drawbacks that come with all of these extra goodies? There sure are. First off, you can't just "sign up" with one of these distributors in the same way you would with an online service. Any artist can start a TuneCore account in just a few minutes. Conversely, you will need to be at least somewhat established before even the smallest full-service distributors will get involved with you. Moreover, your distribution arrangement with one of these organizations will involve a complicated contract rather than a simple online signup. This means you will need to hire a lawyer to review the language. A lawyer will make sure the terms are fair to you and that you are not giving up anything too valuable (such as the ownership of your copyrights) by entering into the deal.

Full service distribution deals are also more expensive than online services. In exchange for receiving a more impressive menu of services, you will likely pay commissions that are more than double what you would pay with a company like CD Baby.

Song Publishing

No discussion of content would be complete without going over the basics of song publishing. Song publishing refers to the exploitation of the copyrights in the songs you write. When you write an original musical composition, you receive a copyright in that song as soon as you "fix" it onto a "tangible medium of expression" (to quote the Copyright Act). This means that as soon as you write the song onto a sheet of paper, record it, or do something else which embodies your song onto a permanent medium, you receive exclusive rights regarding that song. These rights include the right to make copies of your song, to perform your song in public, and to make derivative works of your song (such as making your song into a recording).

You Need to Write Songs

A song copyright is extraordinarily valuable. Having one gives you a monopoly on all profit-making uses of that particular work. Basically, no one can exploit your song in any fashion without your permission as the copyright holder (which you can license for a price). If someone wants to record your song, they have to pay you. If someone wants to perform your song or play it on the radio, they have to pay you. This can mean big money if you write a song which resonates with the public. If your music empire achieves great success, it will be because you managed to create a significant number of income-generating musical compositions.

The revenue potential of song publishing has significant implications for your music operation. Heed these words: If you want to succeed as an independent artist-entrepreneur, <u>you have to be able to write your own songs</u>. Period. Independent artists in today's industry simply cannot make enough money if they are unable to compose their own material. Not only are these artists losing out on the income streams that result from song copyrights, but they have to pay big dollars to other songwriters for the rights to record and perform their material. It is not a winning financial proposition.

Are there exceptions to my blanket statement? Possibly, but you almost assuredly won't be one of them. "But Ryan," you exclaim "I may not be a songwriter, but I have an <u>amazing</u> voice!" I bet you do. And there are plenty of people with amazing voices who can also write amazing songs who are still struggling to achieve success. Getting to the top of this industry is hard enough even if you have all of the tools. If you can't write, it is going to be nearly impossible for you to become a successful artist. This is not to say a non-songwriter cannot make a musical living in other ways (such as by playing in a wedding cover band or working as a backup singer/musician), but you cannot build a music empire without compositions.

If you cannot write, *learn* how to write. Join songwriters' cooperatives to refine your skills, if you must. Failing that, you can also partner with a songwriter, or join a larger band in which someone else in the group does the writing, so that someone within your music operation is writing material.

Making the Most of Your Publishing

To maximize the value of your song publishing, there are some important administrative things that you have to do.

Song registration

The initial step is to register your copyrights in your songs, and continue to register new songs as you create them. While formal registration is not required to have a valid copyright, going through the process gives you strong legal protection in the event that someone steals your work. If you register a work before infringement happens, it puts you in a very strong position when it comes to someone challenging your ownership. Moreover, registered works are entitled to additional damages in an infringement suit.

And to reiterate something from Chapter 4: The "poor man's copyright" of mailing your songs to yourself is *not* a substitute for a valid government registration. Spend the $35 dollars and give your song the true protection that only comes with actual registration. Or, better yet, protect multiple songs with one $35 payment by registering all of them as a "compilation work." Visit the copyright.gov website to complete this fairly painless registration process.

157

Publishing administration

Once your registered songs start to get a little bit of traction, you will want to get an administrator to track the uses of your works throughout the world and to collect the payments due to you. An effective publishing administrator will perform the following services:

- Help you register your works in other countries.
- Help affiliate you with Performance Rights Organizations (such as ASCAP or BMI in the United States, and international PROs as well) so that you can get royalties when your songs are performed in public around the world (such as on the radio or in live music venues).
- Collect royalties from those who want to make and sell recordings of your songs, stream your songs online, sell sheet music, or make ringtones.
- Collect synchronization fees and other royalties from those who want to put your songs in videos (e.g., movies, TV, or YouTube).

In return for these services, your administrator will take a fee, usually somewhere in the range of 10-15% of what they collect. When choosing an administrator, do not forget our golden rule of purchasing services for your career: Do *not* give up your copyrights. You can give them a percentage of what they collect, but not a percentage of the compositions. If a publishing entity wants a piece of your copyrights in exchange for their services, run away.

Song Pluggers

Getting songs placed into a movie, television show, commercial, website, or other media can be a highly lucrative for an artist. When such a placement occurs, the licensor of the content usually pays a "synch fee" for the right to use the artist's song and sound recording in video content. Then, once the media is created, the owner of the song receives royalties every time the content (with the song) is presented to the public. These royalties can add up, particularly if the song is featured in a widely-released film or becomes a theme song for a long-running TV show.

To put it another way, if you ever run into a member of The Rembrandts (who wrote and recorded the theme to the show *Friends*), ask them to buy you a drink. Believe me, they can afford it.

How does one get their material onto these media sources? You need to work with a "song plugging" organization that can connect your material to those looking for music for their production. These companies maintain a database of songs that video content creators can access when looking for music. They will often send catalogues regularly to top music supervisors who are always looking for new synching material.

However, the best pluggers are the ones who actively promote your songs and work aggressively to find placements for you. A few of my clients have had success with the company Jingle Punks, but there are other good ones out there too. Feel free to work with more than one plugger (but if you do, be sure not to give exclusive rights to any single plugger).

A few tips when it comes to song pluggers:

- As always, never work with a company that wants a piece of your copyrights.
- Try to find the ones that are selective with their clients. If the plugger is willing to take anyone's song, then chances are they are not going to give your song special attention.
- Once you sign up with a song plugger, make yourself memorable at that organization. Reach out to the organization regularly, stop by their office when you are in the area, ask the employees out for coffee, and volunteer to play your material at their office. You want to make sure your music is fresh in your plugger's mind when the next big TV opportunity comes through the door.

One last thing: If you want to work with a song plugger like Jingle Punks, make sure that you don't sign a publishing administration deal in which you give exclusive placement rights (including synch opportunities) to your administrator. Some admin companies (such as TuneCore's publishing administration arm) require that you give them the sole right to make placements.

Usually, these administrators will not pay as much attention to finding synch opportunities for your material as a devoted song plugger would. I recommend the company Songtrust if you are looking for a publishing administrator that will not touch your placement rights.

Final Note: Expand Your Definition of Content

This is a book for musicians. Thus, in a chapter about content, it is only natural that the focus will be on music recordings and compositions. But never forget that the job descriptions are blurring more and more in the entertainment industry. Comedians often act in TV sitcoms. Sitcom stars often act in movies. Movie stars often make albums. And musicians, well, they seem to do a little bit of everything. You are a creative soul with a diverse set of artistic interests. It would serve your career well to have your content creation efforts reflect that. Your content can be much more than just music.

Give some thought to all of the artistic pursuits at which you excel and don't be afraid to create content in any and all of those areas. Doing so will expand your revenue streams, increase the value of your brand, and promote fan engagement. Do you like to write fiction? Write a novel or some short stories and self-publish. Do you paint? Paint a new picture every month and put it on your website for sale. Can you act? Reach out to a theatrical agent and go on some auditions. Do you have interesting opinions and like to talk? Create a podcast. The content does not even have to make money directly to advance your career. If it promotes you as an artist-entrepreneur, it is likely worth doing.

Musicians who do other artistic things are more the rule than the exception these days. I have worked with musicians who are also authors, actors, models, dancers, podcasters, voice-over artists, graphic designers, clothing designers, poets, painters, and much more. They are all resourceful professionals who know the value of content, regardless of its form. And they never miss any opportunity to add something new to our popular culture.

CHAPTER 12

YOUR VIDEOS

The Revolution Within the Revolution

Something really wild has happened in the music industry over the last few years.

To be fair, the industry is already in the midst of a revolution with the rise of the Internet and digital distribution. But within that revolution, there is something happening that is particularly radical. It is a phenomenon that is forever changing the rules of content creation, distribution, and promotion. It is an empowering force for artists and a threat to the big-media gatekeepers. It provides thousands of hours of new content for music consumers every single day—and that number will assuredly increase exponentially as time goes on. This phenomenon, this revolution within the revolution, is streaming video. Making the most of this innovative asset is critical to your success as an artist-entrepreneur. Thus, this book has an entire chapter devoted just to creating video content.

This is not the first time that video has caused a sea change in the industry. In 1979, The Buggles famously proclaimed through song that "video killed the radio star," denoting the emergence of music videos on television as a disruptive force in the industry. In the new century, video has found its way onto the Internet and is poised to "kill" some more longstanding institutions in the process. Record labels, traditional distributors, and high-priced music promotion entities may all be on borrowed time now that musicians have access to a worldwide video audience. Creating effective content for this audience is a necessary step to achieving a truly successful independent career.

Though many sites exist for artists to post videos online, this chapter will focus principally on using, creating videos for, and uploading videos to, YouTube. YouTube is the largest video sharing website by far and it is the third-most visited website on the Internet overall. Nearly all of the biggest artists use YouTube, and many successful musicians got their start by posting videos on the site.

As noted in the previous chapter, YouTube will be a critical part of your distribution strategy in the early stages of your career.

Even if you do not consider yourself a "video" artist, you will still need to use the site. The free worldwide distribution YouTube provides is just too valuable to pass up. You need to prioritize creating visual content in addition to your audio material.

Types of Videos

When using YouTube, many musicians fall into the trap of merely using the site as a place to post their traditional music videos. They simply create a channel and fill it with a small handful of basic video content. Maybe, if they are feeling slightly more ambitious, they might throw a few pieces of live concert footage on there. Either way, they treat their YouTube use like a box to check off: "They say I need an Internet video presence? No problem! I'll post my two music videos on there. Done. Mission accomplished!"

Don't make this mistake. If you are a fledgling musician, YouTube is your friend. In fact, scratch that: YouTube is your best friend, soul mate, and devoted life partner. YouTube is giving you free, worldwide promotion and content distribution. It is directly connecting you with over a billion potential consumers. If you are not frequently posting YouTube videos, you are basically saying "No, thanks" to an incredibly valuable free gift. And by turning down this gift, you are depriving yourself of a necessary asset for growing your entertainment organization.

Remain mindful of the last chapter's ABC rule for your content: Always Be Creating. This absolutely applies to your video content as well. Your fans will have an insatiable desire for enjoyable content, and streaming video is an excellent medium to deliver it to them. If you make the right kind of videos, you can expose new people to your music. You can give people an efficient way to share your talents with their friends. You can allow people to experience you in a wide variety of contexts and situations. You can remove any barriers that prevent your fans from learning who you are and why they should like you.

These are all critical goals for you to achieve. Reaching these goals requires that you gain familiarity with the various types of videos that artists can create on sites like YouTube. Each of these video types serves different purposes for you and requires different strategies to execute effectively. To make the most of what YouTube

162

offers, you need to upload more than just typical music videos. You can, and must, do so much more. Here are some of the types of videos you can create:

Home Performance Videos

A great way to distribute your content and show off your talents to the masses is simply to record a video of you performing your song at home (or some other simple location) and posting the video on YouTube. Most emerging artist-entrepreneurs are getting their start by recording and uploading home performances of their material and inviting others to share the video on social media sites. It is undoubtedly the fastest and easiest way to record and distribute your music to the masses.

Live Performance Videos

Do you have a killer live show? Record some gig clips and upload them. Live performance videos can be a particularly useful undertaking. Not only do those clips provide additional opportunities for people to hear your music, but a video featuring screaming fans enjoying your music can motivate others to see you live.

The drawback to these videos is that they often have quality problems. The worst offenders are the ones recorded on a smartphone by someone in the audience. If you record a live video this way, the resulting product will likely be five minutes of crowd noise and only the faintest traces of your performance. Moreover, the obstructed view of an audience vantage point will mean that your fans will see less of you and more of the bald spot of the guy in the front row.

Don't subject your viewers to this kind of video. Make sure your camera(s) have a clear shot of the crowd. Position your recording microphones toward the stage and either above or to the side of the crowd. Or just record the audio straight from the gig's soundboard.

Whichever approach you take, make sure that your live performance video is actually worth watching. If you don't yet have the resources to make a good-quality live video, then you are better off sticking with recordings that take place in a more controlled environment (like home performances).

Traditional Music Videos

For over three decades, nearly every famous recording artist has used the music video format as a valuable promotional tool. And with the rise of the Internet and sites like YouTube, music videos have only grown in importance. Today, consumers can watch music videos on demand and send them to their friends instantaneously. No longer burdened by the strictures of a television schedule, music videos have much more reach now than when they were played twenty-four hours a day on networks like MTV and VH1. (Do you even remember those days? You might not have even been born yet. Now I feel old.)

Your YouTube channel would be well served by having some music videos on it. When you start out, your first music videos will likely be simple, inexpensive undertakings. Modest projects like a lyric video or a slideshow of pictures synched with one of your recordings can give you good content without exhausting your limited resources. And as you start to build your career and you have some money to spend, you can begin to take on more ambitious projects. Later in this chapter, you will learn more about how to make these sorts of videos in a fiscally responsible fashion.

Non-Music Productions

In these videos, you will give your audience the opportunity to enjoy your diverse artistic talents. You are a creative soul and you almost assuredly have abilities outside of making and performing music. Exploiting those abilities in video form is a great way to promote yourself as a general entertainment personality, increase fan engagement, and ultimately draw people to your music content (particularly if you include your music content as background in these videos).

These videos can be regular segments that you post frequently or one-time productions. Do what you feel works best for you and your career. Here are just some of the non-music video productions that artist-entrepreneurs like you have done on YouTube.

- A weekly vlog
- Regular readings of original poetry
- A cooking webseries
- Weekly makeup tips
- Movie reviews
- Long-form interviews with other musicians
- "Making of" featurettes for music videos
- A series of painting lessons
- A monthly segment on choosing the right music equipment
- Dance videos
- Workout videos
- A weekly fan mail segment

Random Video Uploads

A couple years ago, I was riding in a hotel elevator with a musician client. It was the night of an award show, and we were heading to the lobby to await our ride to the venue. We were silent as I was watching the digital floor readout count down. Then suddenly, out of nowhere, my colleague started shouting: "Hey everyone! What's up? I'm here in the hotel getting ready for the big night! I'm really excited to perform on the broadcast and I hope you all tune in to check it out. Thank you for your support. I love you all!"

I turned my head toward him, quite confused. Was my client rehearsing what he was going to say to his fans downstairs? Had he simply lost his mind and was talking to imaginary people?

I saw that he was holding up his iPhone and quickly realized that he was recording a quick video. "What are you going to do with that?" I asked.

"Post it. Twitter and Facebook."

"Your fans want to watch you stand in an elevator?"

"Stand in an elevator. Walk around my neighborhood. Hang out in the studio. I make these little videos all the time. Each one gets a ton of views. My people like seeing what I am up to and hearing little messages from me," he answered.

He never missed an opportunity to record something. Thirty minutes later, he filmed another quick clip for his devotees. This time, it was just before he left the car to walk the red carpet.

After going online and seeing the tremendous fan engagement each of these posts generated, I realized that my client understood how to make the most of the video medium. His audience of teens and tweens loved keeping constant tabs on their heartthrob, and he was more than happy to give them what they wanted. These videos helped him cultivate a massive base of die-hards eager to buy his music and promote him vociferously throughout cyberspace. I started the evening thinking my client was a crazy person who liked to yell in elevators. I ended it understanding that he was, in fact, a promotional genius.

The above story epitomizes one of the most intriguing aspects of Internet videos. Not every recording you make has to be a structured, organized piece of content, like a music video or a weekly vlog. Instead, many artists have realized that they also can make random videos which chronicle their life as a performer. These little clips are a powerful promotional tool. They allow people to get closer than ever to the artists they love.

Your fans want to get to know you, and they will reward you handsomely if you let them. Thus, your video strategy should include random, unstructured videos. Show them a few minutes of your band rehearsing. Let them see you throwing Frisbees during a Saturday barbecue. Give them a video tour of your new apartment. They will love it! You can even use an app like Periscope to stream out live videos of yourself on your smartphone and let your fans interact with you in real time.

Just make sure that you keep your videos interesting. Just because you are showing them random events of your career does not mean that these events should be boring. Try to keep them short and sweet; don't let them drag.

And be sure to keep the unique characteristics of your audience in mind when producing your random videos. My client's young, boy-crazy, Twitter-addicted fans loved seeing several clips a day from their idol. If your fans skew older and have different sensibilities, they might prefer not to see your face every couple hours. A daily video might work better for them.

166

Equipment for Professional-Looking Videos

There are many artist-entrepreneurs out there already taking advantage of streaming video to further their careers. This means that you are entering a crowded field and you will need to take concrete steps to stand out. One way to help achieve this goal is to make your videos look professionally produced. The equipment used in the vast majority of artist videos consists of a simple camera and nothing more. If you can make even slight upgrades to this baseline, you can go a long way in creating content that people want to see. And luckily, you can obtain a lot of these professional trappings without paying a professional price. Here are some of the items worth obtaining:

Camera

It should go without saying that you will need a good camera to create your video projects. Since you will be posting your videos on the web, your first impulse might be to use your computer's built-in camera to make your video content. After all, you will use your computer to upload the video, so why not use that same computer to record as well? Here's why not: Your computer's built-in camera probably stinks. Don't feel bad; I'm not insulting your computer-purchasing skills. I have just yet to encounter a built-in that I would trust for anything other than the most basic recording projects. The quality tends to be awful, and zooming in or out is not really an option. Besides, do you really want to record yourself on the same camera you use for all your grainy, pixelated Skype calls?

Instead, look elsewhere for affordable camera options. Many of the cameras on modern smartphones have incredible quality, and I have seen artists make some good content with them. You can also use a DSLR camera. DSLRs are "still" cameras that can also take great video, and they are small and easy to transport. Since you will need to take many photographs in your entertainment career anyway, a good DSLR is a smart investment. You can buy used ones for a reasonable price online and use the cost savings to grab some useful accessories (e.g., lenses, filters, tripod, battery pack, and memory card).

Down the road, you can certainly buy yourself a professional video camera once you have the means to do so. That being said, you will be surprised with the results you can get in the meantime with the more affordable options above.

Recording Audio in Your Video

When making video content, the "video" aspect is only one half of the equation. Your audience needs to hear you, too. Nothing ruins a potentially good video faster than bad sound quality. Your audience may be willing to forgive mediocre visuals, but they will have no patience for quiet, static-riddled, echoing audio. Unfortunately, many artist videos tend to feature such sound, which all but guarantees that those works will not be significantly viewed or shared.

The main culprit of bad sound? Usually, it happens because the artist tries to use whatever microphone is attached to their camera to record audio. Such a microphone might get the job done if you are recording something simple—like a check-in to your fans in a hotel elevator. But anything more ambitious will require extra equipment for a good final product. Attached microphones are almost always of poor quality. And the biggest problem with them is that they're, well, attached. They are permanently grafted to your recording device instead of being near the person actually emitting sound. As a result, the mic winds up picking up a lot more air and a lot less you.

Here are some better audio recording options:

1. External Microphones - For videos where you are just trying to record yourself talking, these work great. Hand-held external microphones are good if you don't mind holding something during the video. If you want to keep your hands free, get a livelier "lapel" mic or a boom mic. You can connect your mic straight into the camera. Or, if you want better results, record your audio on a separate device and edit everything together after the fact. The latter technique is a little more complicated. Be sure you learn how to do it effectively before you start regularly making videos this way.

2. Record Audio Feed - If you are trying to record multiple instruments in a video—particularly if some of those instruments are

electric—you are better off running your audio through a soundboard and recording straight from there.

3. Use Pre-Existing Audio – If you are making a traditional music video, you will undoubtedly use audio you have already recorded and mastered beforehand. In these situations, you shouldn't have any significant audio recording issues on the actual day of shooting. One less worry for you!

Lighting

Good lighting is critical to creating videos with professional-looking production values, especially when shooting indoors. In fact, a well-crafted lighting setup can make your recorded visuals look big-budget even if you had to skimp on your actual camera.

To create a good lighting setup, "three point lighting" is usually the best way to go. Three-point lighting consists of: (1) a "key light" to the left of the camera, (2) a "fill light" on the right side of the camera to remove shadows caused by the key light, and (3) a "back light" positioned behind and above the subject to make them look less flat. Some video makers also like to use a "ring light," which is a bright "O"-shaped light positioned directly in front of the camera. The ring light's 360-degree design allows it to serve the purpose of the first two lights in close-up shots, or act as a supplement to a three-point setup for longer shots.

Lighting can be expensive. Even a moderately professional three-point kit (with ring light) will cost in the neighborhood of $1,000 or more. Until you have that kind of money, you will need to get by with a more jury-rigged setup. Three adjustable desk lamps with 65-watt fluorescent bulbs can serve as your three points until you can afford the real thing. It is not a permanent solution, but it will allow you to start making decent videos at a minimal startup cost. As you are setting up your three points, play around with different angles until you get your desired lighting effect. You might prefer different lighting "looks" for different types of videos.

Editing

Once you have recorded a visually impressive, aurally pleasant, and well-lit video masterpiece, now comes the most important part: editing everything together. Everything above your most simple recording projects will likely involve at least some editing. A generation ago, the technology required for professional-quality editing was beyond most indie musicians' reach. Editing software and hardware used to be expensive to obtain and difficult to use.

Today, artists like you can edit damn good videos on a basic laptop (and possibly even a tablet or smartphone!). To edit your videos, I recommend software like the program Final Cut. You can do a lot with it and the learning curve is not too steep. YouTube even has its own web-based editor, which can work in a pinch. And if video editing is just not your thing, or your time is too valuable to edit videos yourself, you can certainly outsource this task to others over the Internet using a site like Fiverr.com.

Making Good Music Videos on a Budget

Your most difficult video undertakings will be your traditional music videos of one of your songs, assuming you are doing something more elaborate than a simple lyric video. These projects can involve lots of pre-production and may require the assistance of many individuals. There will be heavy editing involved, particularly if your video has multiple cuts and you are shooting at more than one location. A professional music video can be a great addition to your content catalog, but they can also be really expensive to put together. Luckily, there are a couple of things that artists like you frequently do to make high-quality videos at a reasonable cost.

For one thing, making a good music video on a budget means keeping your concept simple. "You gotta know your parameters," notes C.T. Fields of indie band Lovebettie. "If money is tight, you're not going to have a sports car in your video or have something explode." Singer-songwriter Natalie Gelman echoes similar sentiment: "In my first video we just filmed me playing piano in a rehearsal room. It was simple but it looked great." There is nothing wrong with a modest concept for your music video. If anything, it allows your music to be the central focus of the work.

Moreover, you need to find resourceful ways to make big-ticket items more affordable. If you hire a videographer to help you with your video, they can provide a lot of the recording equipment for you and may even take care of editing. Of course, this means that you still have to pay for the videographer, which can be really pricey unless you get creative. Gelman recommends that artists seek out film students in their area who might need to make a music video for a class project. Fields uses another approach: He advises that artists network with other bands in their area that also want to make their own video. Then, he recommends, all the bands should reach out to one videographer collectively and negotiate a package deal where the videographer works on all of the videos at a discounted bulk rate. "It is a win-win for everyone," notes Fields. "We get a video for ourselves, we get a video for all of our friends who are in bands, we get to network with other musicians, and the videographer makes good money."

Covering Songs in Your Videos

Many artist-entrepreneurs like to create video content by covering another artist's song in a home performance video. Your YouTube subscribers would likely enjoy watching you perform other people's material in your unique style. Cover videos can help draw people to your original music and increase your fan base. Many successful artists—like Justin Bieber, Karmin, Boyce Avenue, and Grayson Chance—got their start by making these sorts of videos.

Despite the prevalence and effectiveness of these videos, I do wish to impart a word of caution: Most artists make these cover videos without the permission of the original song's copyright holder. If you do the same, you are infringing on a valid copyright unless the copyright holder has given permission for their songs to be covered in this manner. If you make a cover of a copyrighted song without permission, you are almost surely violating federal law. The copyright holder (which is usually the song's writer and/or publishing company) has the exclusive right to decide who can synchronize their song with a video, and who can cover and distribute their song through streaming video. By making a cover video and posting it to YouTube, you are violating all of those rights.

Now, do I agree with this part of the law? Absolutely not. In a perfect world, these sorts of covers would not be considered infringing. Copyright holders are not significantly hurt by up-and-coming artists making what are essentially video tributes. If anything, these videos often serve to increase the popularity of the original artist.

And will you get sued if you make a cover video? Probably not (but the possibility always exists). If a copyright holder wants to put a stop to your video, the more likely scenario is that they will just send a notice-and-takedown to YouTube, and your infringing content will simply disappear from the site. YouTube also tends to delete the accounts of repeat infringers.

So what should you do? More and more publishers are striking deals with YouTube that allow their songs to be used on the site in exchange for advertising revenue. Unfortunately, there is no easy way to find out which songs have that clearance. You can also try reaching out to the publisher and their rights management agency for the appropriate licenses, but their fee might be out of your price range. So, until a better solution arises for emerging artists, you might consider limiting your covers to songs in the public domain. Perhaps you could put your unique spin on a traditional holiday standard, or modernize a piece from a bygone era.

Getting Lots of Views

To close out this chapter, here are some final pieces of advice to help make your videos gain traction on the Internet:

Don't Forget The "Jellybeans"

One of my favorite music videos ever made is by acoustic-pop artist Kina Grannis. In 2011, Grannis released the music video for her song "In Your Arms." In the video, she sings her song in front of a stop-motion background made up of thousands of jellybeans. The jellybeans change color, form images, and even create characters with which she interacts. It is a marvelous video. And though the actual "In Your Arms" song is delightful, it is Kina's magic jellybeans which made the video go viral. Chances are at least one of your social medial friends shared it with a caption along the lines of "Cool! Check out these jellybeans!"

The YouTube views for "In Your Arms" have reached eight figures, demonstrating an important principle of making video content: Your content needs a hook to go viral. Even if you have a lot of talent and your underlying material is great, you still need that special something that catches people's attention. A great video makes people think, "Wow, great video." A great video with a hook makes people think, "Wow, great video. <u>I need to tweet this out!</u>" And that makes all of the difference.

If you want lots of views for a video—whether it is a music video, a home performance, non-music content, or even a random post—you need a hook. Your videos need something unique and intriguing that makes people want to share you with their friends. Kina Grannis had her jellybeans. The band OK Go danced on treadmills. Scott Bradlee performs modern songs in old musical styles. As you make your videos, think about how you could produce your content with an element that catches people's attention and makes them want to pass along your video to others.

Partner With Other Artists

A great way to get extra views, expand your fan base, and network with other entertainment professionals is to make video content with other musicians. It will open you up to another universe of viewers, particularly ones who are in your co-collaborator's demographic group or geographic area. Moreover, nothing says that your collaboration partners always have to be musicians. As Natalie Gelman notes, "I once met a girl while I was busking who made YouTube videos where she gave make-up tips. I let her use my song in one of her videos and at the end she said 'Please go subscribe to Natalie, she's awesome.' I got 400 subscribers overnight!"

Using Online Resources, From YouTube and Elsewhere

Here are a few online techniques you can use to boost your subscribers:

1. Directly asking for subscriptions in your video, either directly, by adding a "coda" to the end of your video, or by inserting annotation bubbles in your video.

2. Searching for people on YouTube who are interested in your style of music and messaging them directly.

3. Using a service like TubeAssist to automatically share your videos with targeted viewers and to add additional contacts.

4. Posting your videos to your website and social media pages. Or, better yet, use a program that does this for you automatically.

5. Interact with others on YouTube. If you want people to take interest in your content, then take an interest in the content of others and be an active part of this amazing community of content creators.

Your Content Has to Speak For Itself

In the end, all of your hooks, artist collaboration, and aggressive video promotion will get you nowhere if you have lousy content. Make sure you are producing stuff that people actually want to watch and share with their friends. Take pride in the videos you produce; they are the way that most people are initially going to get to know you and your music.

Monetization

Streaming video will be an important aspect of promoting your entertainment career. It will be the initial way that most people hear your music and see the person who created it. But if you become particularly adept at making good videos, this medium can do more than just promote your career. It can be a revenue-generating enterprise. Top video creators can join YouTube's Partner Program, allowing them to get a cut of advertising dollars from their videos. Putting product placements in videos is an option as well. You could even create a way for your fans to help finance each video you create by using a site like Patreon. Lots of monetization options are available to you if your video fame reaches a certain level, and those options are only increasing with time.

CHAPTER 13

YOUR PROMOTION

The World is Yours, If You're Willing to Work For It

By now, I am hoping that you are seeing a theme emerge from the last two chapters: The Internet and the digital revolution have leveled the playing field in the music industry. We are experiencing a phenomenon that has taken leverage away from typical record companies and has empowered independent artists.

Chapters 11 and 12 discussed how the Internet and new technology have made content creation and distribution a low-cost endeavor. You can create almost any sort of art and show it to anyone in the world without needing some big company to front you the money (and ultimately siphon your earnings). Multi-million dollar recording studios are being replaced by laptop computers. Distribution trucks have become obsolete thanks to fiber optic cable. Retail store purchases have given way to finger taps on smartphones. Achieving success as an entertainer used to be expensive and complex. Today, you can create art and share it widely for practically nothing—and you can often do it without even leaving your house.

This incredible technological power allows you to bring your content to the world independently. But there is still an important question you need to answer to achieve your success: How do you ensure that the world is actually paying attention? Can you use these same tech resources to *promote* your content as effectively as you create and distribute it?

Indeed, you can.

In the old music industry model, music promotion was a costly proposition. Terrestrial radio campaigns, promotional appearances, and TV and print advertising were the standard practice. But in this new industry, this independent and artist-centered industry, free Internet resources allow all musicians to achieve worldwide promotion. And they can do it without shackling themselves to a record label machine.

As an independent artist-entrepreneur, the Internet will serve as the centerpiece of your promotional activities. You will use social media and your website to raise awareness of your entertainment operation. If you use these resources effectively and to their fullest capability, you can work toward making yourself a household name without spending a fortune.

There's just one catch: Since these powerful promotional resources are basically free, that means that *every* artist has access to them. The Internet has leveled the playing field for you, but it also leveled it for all musicians. Anyone can set up a Twitter account or build a website. So if you want to cut through the clutter and ensure your voice is heard, you need to *hustle*. You need to outwork your fellow artists. You need to post, tweet, blog, email, and interact constantly. These activities need to become as natural for you as breathing—and occur almost as frequently.

Your promotional contributions have to be interesting as well. If your social media profiles are filled with nothing but concert announcements, sparse news updates, and links to your webpage, then you are missing the point. You need to use this technology to let people get to know you. You need to let yourself become a constant presence in their online lives. Your fans don't just want to hear your music; they want to feel invested in your development as an artist and as a person. Internet promotion allows them to watch you grow—to watch you bring your art into this world.

They want pictures of you. They want videos of you. They want blog entries. They want to ask questions about you and have them answered. They want to know what music and TV shows you like. They want to learn about you as a person. They want to know your general life philosophy. And if you let them in on these things, then they will reward you with their devotion (and dollars).

Types of Social Media

For independent musicians, social media is a giant mountain of awesome. These platforms allow artists to have a free, never-ending, and worldwide promotional campaign for their careers. And they can create and maintain this campaign from their laptop or smartphone. But despite the unlimited potential of this phenomenon, a great many of today's independent artists do not make adequate use of social media. I have seen far too many performers with threadbare Facebook pages, or who tweet only a

176

handful of times a month (or year!), or whose Instagram features just a couple of photos from a single live show they did three years ago. If you squander these valuable resources, your career will assuredly fail. Social media is not an option for emerging musicians—it is a requirement.

Here is a list of social media platforms that you should consider making part of your promotion strategy. One important thing to keep in mind regarding this list is that it is by no means exhaustive. The sites shown below are the ones that my clients predominantly use, but there are plenty of others out there. Moreover, the social media landscape is always changing (I know at least a few of you are looking at my list and thinking, "How did he not mention [your favorite new platform]?!"). New platforms are constantly emerging and the graveyard of now-defunct sites continues to grow. You should always keep your eyes open for the next big thing.

Facebook – is the largest social media platform in the world and the second most-visited website on the Internet. On Facebook, people create profiles to connect with and meet new friends. The site also allows artists to create profiles to promote their careers to Facebook's 1.3 billion users. Creating a profile offers artists an opportunity to describe themselves and their music to potential fans. Moreover, artists can also talk to fans directly over Facebook (by either messaging them directly or posting on the fan's profile page) and post status updates, links, photos, music, and other content on the site.

Twitter – is a social media site that allows users to post quick updates ("tweets") to people who "follow" them on the site. Twitter is exceedingly popular with top recording artists, the most famous of whom have tens of millions of followers on the site. Relative to Facebook, Twitter is a much more stripped-down interface: Twitter profiles provide much less information about the user. Moreover, the site imposes a 140-character limit for tweets (but you can also post pictures and video). Twitter is for quick bursts of information about your career developments. Users look to the site for fast updates on everyone they are following.

177

Instagram – is a photo sharing social media site that allows its users to post photos and short videos on their Instagram page as well as share them on other social media sites. Part of Instagram's appeal stems from its photo filter features, which allows users to add different artistic effects to their pictures.

Pinterest – is a social media site in which users set up a virtual "pinboard" where they can post images, links, videos, and other "pins." Users can browse other users' pinboards, which are grouped by category. The main point of Pinterest is to help its users discover content relating to their interests. However, the site also allows people to discover the interests of other users. This is where this website can be of particular value to musicians trying to promote themselves to their fans. Pinterest gives you a valuable opportunity to show your fans a more complete picture of who you are. For example, Nashville-based indie singer-songwriter Mary Jennings uses her pinboard to foster deeper fan engagement: "I posted my own recipe for laundry detergent on Pinterest. People ask why I would post about that. Well, fans are curious and they make my recipe. Now every single time they do their laundry they're thinking 'Oh, this is Mary Jennings' recipe. She's a musician. That's cool.' That person has now been thinking about me for hours, instead of just listening to me for a three-minute song."

Email Lists – Though technically not a form of social media, email lists serve many of the same functions and thus warrant inclusion in this section. Email lists were a social outlet for musicians before social media was even a thing. Before Facebook and Twitter, artists could reach their fans directly by obtaining email addresses from fans and sending out updates to their mailing list. Even though email lists are more antiquated than modern social media platforms, artist manager Eric Sussman (Amanda Palmer) advises artists not to abandon them just yet: "For certain artists, depending on their demographic, mailing lists remain one of the strongest methods of reaching a large number of people, your people, the people who are committed to you. Maintain your list and constantly keep it updated." Many independent artists continue to swear by this tried-and-true communication method, and you probably should as well. Besides, it's not like email is going anywhere anytime soon.

Other Social Media Worth Considering - LinkedIn (for business networking), Google+ (general social media), SoundCloud (social media and music discovery), SplashFlood (social media and music discovery), Last.fm (social media and music discovery), MySpace (social media with a music emphasis), ReverbNation (social media and music discovery), Tumblr (social media and microblogging).

A Successful Social Media Strategy

The major social media platforms all do different things well. Facebook broadcasts your information to a wide audience. Twitter distributes quick thoughts efficiently. Instagram tells your visual story. Pinterest shows the world your unique tastes and affinities. Given that each of these sites have their own strengths, the best course is to incorporate more than one in your social media strategy.

For whatever platforms you use, be sure to study up on the particulars of each site to learn how to use them to their full potential. And with regard to your social media strategy as a whole, there are some good general best practices to follow:

Autopost Your Social Media Content

When something happens in your career that you want to share, you may want to make it known on more than one social media platform. But it can be quite time-consuming to log into each of your sites and post the same information over and over. It would be inefficient to share a picture of yourself by taking it on Instagram, logging into Twitter to tweet it out, and then scooting over to Facebook to post it to your wall. As you may very well make several social media updates each day, posting to each page separately would be quite a time suck.

To solve this problem, use programs that can "autopost" your content onto multiple platforms. One way to do this is by linking your Facebook profile to your other social media pages. For example, Facebook allows its users to "link" different social media pages together so that their Facebook posts can also appear on sites like Twitter or ReverbNation.

Another way to handle autoposting is to use a separate social media management program like Hootsuite.com. Posting to multiple platforms through Facebook can get a little cumbersome. You are limited by Facebook's functionality and reluctance to help you post to competing platforms. Instead, with Hootsuite, you can manage all of your platforms using a single separate interface. This makes autoposting a breeze. You can manage up to three social media sites and two blogs on Hootsuite for free as part of its basic package. Hootsuite even has a smartphone app, allowing you to manage your promotional content even if you are not near a computer.

Post Frequently and Keep it Interesting

As discussed earlier in this chapter, posting on social media needs to become a frequent exercise for you. Denizens of the Internet have short attention spans. You will likely have to make at least one or more social media post each day to drive your career. One of my musician friends posts daily to Facebook and Twitter and "Instagrams" a new picture every week. Another friend posts on all of his social media pages 3-4 times each day. I even have a client who tweets a dozen times a day or more. If you do post multiple times each day, be sure to spread your posts out. Let some time pass between updates to give your fans time to digest new information. If you use Hootsuite, you can set it to "schedule" posts for a specific date and time to prevent your social media activity from clumping together.

You might be wondering how you can possibly come up with several posts a day worth of content. It is understandable if you are concerned that you won't have enough updates to post— especially if you are just starting out. After all, there are only so many new songs, show announcements, news items, and website updates to report when you are still getting your career off the ground.

To solve this problem, you need to expand the topics of your social media posts beyond your musician activities. Let your followers learn about you, the person, and not just you, the performer. Almost any somewhat-interesting occurrence in your life, even it is not related to your music content, is good social media fodder. Are you on a vacation? Are you eating an interesting meal? Are you reading a good book? Post about it. Did you just see an awesome movie? Are you thinking about a new song idea? Are you at a music store looking to buy a new guitar? Post about it. Does your dog look particularly adorable today? Do you want people to know about another artist you like? Did you find an interesting link online? Post about it! Are you bored waiting in line at the DMV? Let your fans know! They will appreciate the opportunity to relate to a musician they love ("Cool, (s)he hates the DMV too!").

And don't forget the pictures! You can make any social media post significantly more interesting by including a picture. Try to include an accompanying picture with a post whenever you can. Humans are visual creatures. Giving your audience something to look at with your post will guarantee higher-quality engagement. Moreover, pictures draw more attention simply by virtue of the fact that a post with an image occupies additional space on a person's screen. People love to see pictures. You are much more likely to get Facebook "likes" and "favorited" tweets if the post has a visual element. Moreover, visual posts are more likely to be shared by others. Besides, in the age of smartphones, there is no excuse for not posting a ton of pictures. Today, you can take a picture on your phone and use the same phone to post it to social media.

Generally, the more personal and casual the picture is, the better. Make sure that most of your photographs are not polished promo shots done by a professional. This might seem counterintuitive, but high-quality, professional-looking pictures are not the way to go. A constant barrage of polished photos will do more harm than good. Not only are these pictures quite expensive, but they aren't what your fans truly want to see. Your fans want accessibility. They want to be part of your day-to-day experience. Your non-professional pictures help them do that. Your fans would rather see a shot of you hanging out with friends at the beach, or maybe a quick selfie of you backstage at your gig. Granted, a few promo photos are nice to have, but they should not be how you are principally depicting yourself on social media.

If you are looking for more posting ideas, go back to your Strengths and Weaknesses Document from Chapter 10. Review your answers to Questions 40 and 41, in which you outlined your non-music talents and your non-music interests. Those two areas are fertile ground for social media posts. If you can draw, tweet out some nice doodles. If you know magic tricks, post some videos of your best illusions. If you like football, talk about your favorite team's upcoming game. Call upon all of your talents and affinities to keep the fresh posts coming.

Direct Interaction

Posting general updates on your platforms is only part of the equation. It is also critical that you use these sites to speak directly to people. Social media is, at its core, a communication tool. Your followers have to be more than icons on your page; you need to interact with them on a one-on-one basis. It will help you develop a devoted fan base.

Many indie musicians will spend several hours a week talking to fans over social media. You can use Facebook's Messenger app to check in on people who have "liked" your page. You don't need to say anything special to them. A simple "Hi, how's it going?" can start a conversation that ends with you having a more engaged fan. If you are feeling particularly generous, you could send them a free song over Facebook Messenger as a thank you for their appreciation. Twitter is also great for one-on-one conversations. You can use "@ mentions" to target a specific follower with your tweet. Or, if you want to have a private conversation with that follower, you can use Twitter's and Instagram's "DM" (Direct Message) feature.

The time you invest directly communicating with fans can pay big dividends down the road. Chapter 9 outlined the concept of your "Three Fs": Friends, Family, and Fans. People in your Three Fs are the ones who appreciate you enough to help you when you need it (usually for free, or at least at a reduced rate). They will tell their friends about you and help your career in various ways. Direct fan communication is a useful way to move a casual supporter into "Three F" Territory. If you can make strong fans in different geographic areas, you can start building virtual street teams who will happily promote your gigs in their particular hometown.

Crowdsourcing

You can also use social media as a "crowdsourcing" tool. Crowdsourcing refers to the act of soliciting a large group of people to get the things one needs. As a musician, you will frequently need something in a pinch. Reaching out to your fans on social media is a good way to let your fans help you out. In the early stages of Amanda Palmer's independent career, she would often use Twitter to ask for rides from the airport, a place to crash after a show, or a good restaurant recommendation in a particular city. Sometimes she would even bounce songwriting ideas off her fans and get their feedback.

Social media crowdsourcing can be a beneficial activity. As long as you don't abuse it, your fans will usually appreciate the opportunity to help you out. Just make sure that you return the favor. A "thank you" on social media, some free music, and an autograph is the least you can do to repay a generous fan.

It's Not All About You

In a blog post, noted publicist Ariel Hyatt recommended that one should reserve thirty percent of one's social media posts to "shine a light" on others. At first, this might seem odd: Your platforms exist to promote your career, right? Why shouldn't you be the focus of every post?

The problem is that focusing every post on you will make you look like an egomaniac. Your fans want to see you as a human being, and human beings care about people other than themselves. If you want people to like you, you need to show them that you are capable of liking others. Your social media pages are more than just giant virtual billboards for your career; they make you part of a worldwide community. And it is imperative to acknowledge others in that community. Not only will talking about others make you a more interesting follow, but mentioning other people will make those people more likely to mention you in return.

Getting More Likes/Followers/Shares

People are always looking for ways to increase their social media presence. Who wouldn't want to have big numbers? In fact, if you type "How do I get more" into Google, three of the top five autocomplete results are "...followers on Instagram", "...likes on Instagram", and "...followers on Twitter." If you want more social media love, there are a few tricks of the trade you can employ. Make sure you advertise your social media sites in any place that your fans might look. This would include places like your website, YouTube videos, posters, and CD labels.

Our Pinterest queen Mary Jennings uses a few easy techniques to advertise her platforms. She puts all of her social media links on her flyers and business cards so that people in the real world can learn about her virtual presence. Jennings also promotes her pages during live shows: "When I tour with other artists, I will say to the audience 'the first person to tweet at me as soon as I am done playing will get a free CD.'" Finally, when she posts a major announcement on her pages, she will occasionally use Facebook's and Twitter's post-sponsoring tools to spread the word outside of her social media circle. These sponsored posts are not free. But if you have a big enough announcement, it might be worth it to spend the money. A well-executed sponsored post can help you reach new people and bring you more followers.

For the most part, however, your social media growth has to come organically. The above tips will help you a little bit, but in the end there are no shortcuts to getting tons of passionate fans. Most of the artists I work with who are popular on social media got that way with old-fashioned hard work. They post interesting things often, they interact with others, and their career successes make people want to follow them.

One last point on this subject: Don't waste your money on those silly "adding" programs that will get you fake followers. A big number on your pages might give you a tiny ego boost, but it will do nothing for your actual career. Focus less on the quantity of your followers and more on the quality of their engagement. There are plenty of artist-entrepreneurs out there who have great careers with just a few thousand followers. The reason is because a great number of those followers are highly devoted to them. These artists worked very hard to foster strong fan engagement, and it has paid off for them.

Your Website

Another important component to your online promotion is a good website. The finer points of creating an effective artist website could easily fill its own book. That being said, I have collected a few tips from some of the web-savvy musicians with whom I work:

1. When you are starting out, don't spend big money on a professional web designer to create your page. Your resources will be tight in the early going, and you can create a great-looking page just by modifying a pre-existing Wordpress shell and incorporating your logos and artwork.

2. Grab your visitors' attention right away. When a person visits your website, they should be able to know everything important about your career within ten seconds. This means putting all of your major events within the past year on your homepage. Put important things like your videos, touring calendar, merchandise, and photo albums front and center. Include a music player (with links to purchase your music) and your Twitter feed as well. Don't make visitors have to click around to different pages on your site to learn your story. They will likely not have the patience for that. You can certainly have multiple pages on your site, but make sure all of the good stuff is easily accessible on your homepage.

3. Keep the site active and update it constantly. Don't let old news stories and out-of-date show announcements dominate your homepage. It will make you look like your career has stalled (and even if it has, you don't want it to *look* like it has). One way to always guarantee a steady stream of website content is to add the updates from your social media pages to your site.

4. Create a blog. Not only will a regularly-updated blog provide fresh content for your website, but blogs have other benefits for you as well. Blogs give your fans a great opportunity to get to know you on a more personal level. Blog updates also make for great social media posts. You can link to your blog on tweets and

post blog entries in full on Facebook. If you don't like to write, do a video-based "vlog" instead.

5. Make sure your contact information (including your artist e-mail address and social media information) is easy to find on your homepage. Don't make it difficult for listeners, show bookers, journalists, and other industry personnel to reach out to you.

6. Have a nice biography for the "About" section of your website. At a minimum, it should include your history, your style of music (mention artists with a similar sound to yours), and your biggest achievements. Be sure to also place this bio (or at least a shorter version of it) on your social media pages. If you are having trouble writing a bio to your liking, use a site like Fiverr.com to hire someone to write one for you.

7. Use an autoposting tool like Hootsuite.com so that you can easily post any updates to your website (including blog entries) onto your social media platforms.

Some Final Notes on Promotion

From the Virtual World to the Real World

Today, a significant portion of the music industry resides in cyberspace. Consequently, much of your promotion activities will occur there as well. The online promotion tools discussed above are free, effective, and convenient to use. If you can master these virtual platforms, you will go a long way toward making yourself a household name. However, there are also plenty of activities you can do in the real world to help promote yourself as well. Keep your eyes open for non-virtual opportunities to make connections and get breaks. Songwriting conferences, chamber of commerce events, and pop culture/media conventions are all great places to meet people who can help advance your career.

Publicists

The online tools discussed in this chapter will make you more than capable of handling all of your own promotion activity. However, there may be some occasions where you might want a helping hand. When you are undergoing a significant career activity, such as an album release, you might be well served by hiring a publicist. A publicist will put some professional muscle behind your project's promotion, connecting you to media outlets that can give your work valuable press exposure. A good publicist will be able to gauge your music style and career stage to find the outlets that will be most receptive to your project. There are plenty of publicists out there with a significant online presence, such as CyberPR.com. This makes them well-suited to help promote you to online publications.

The drawback to publicists is that they tend to be a little pricey. Most of them require that you pay them up front, and there is no guarantee that their campaign will be successful for you. Think of a hired publicist as icing on your promotional cake. You can achieve a lot on your own using free social media. But if you have the means, investing in an outside professional can be money worth spending.

CHAPTER 14

YOUR FUNDRAISING

A Dollar is What I Need

As discussed throughout this book, the changing dynamics of the music industry has made it easier than ever for artists to pursue careers without subjecting themselves to record company exploitation. Not too long ago, the road to artistic success was paved with label dollars. The funding required to create, distribute, and promote music was beyond the reach of most musicians. A record company's financing was essential to a successful career in music.

Unfortunately, that financing came with many strings attached. In standard deals, labels recoup just about every dollar they spend, and more, from the artist's royalties under the deal. And even though the artist ultimately bears the financial burden of making their records, it is the label that owns all of the copyrights. Moreover, labels also employ 360 clauses to take a sizable chunk of their artists' non-record income, despite the fact that the label usually does very little to actually earn that money. Finally, these companies also use a variety of other terms designed to keep an artist stuck in these nasty deals for many years—even if the label has lost interest in actually making any music with the artist.

But those days are quickly coming to an end. No, record companies have not changed their shady practices. Instead, the industry is changing around them. New technologies have made the recording, distribution, and promotion of music cheaper than ever. Many of these once-expensive music business activities can now be done for free or close to it. Artists no longer need label financing, and all of the undesirable conditions that come with it, to achieve their career goals.

Am I suggesting that a musician can go from zero to superstar without spending any money? Certainly not. Even in the new music industry—the era of iTunes distribution and social media promotion—there are still many things artists need that are not completely free. Moving a music career forward often requires investing in significant projects. Things like EPs, full-length albums, professional-quality music videos, or multi-city tours are important

188

drivers of an artist's operation. These projects are cheaper than they used to be, thanks to modern technology. But they still come with a significant price tag.

Unless you are independently wealthy or have some other access to funding, these sorts of projects likely exceed your means as an emerging artist-entrepreneur. Once you get some career success, it will be easier to fund these big projects out of your own pocket. But how do you get to that point? How do you fund your *first* twelve-track studio album, or your *inaugural* tour, when you don't have much cash in your bank account?

Fortunately, there are ways to bridge this funding gap while still maintaining full independence over your career. You have resources at your disposal that, if used effectively, can provide you the startup funding you need. This chapter will discuss a couple of those resources.

Crowdfunding

Oh, the blessed treasure that is the Internet! It has given musicians so much. This marvelous technology has made music distribution as simple as clicking a mouse. It has given all artists worldwide promotional reach through social media. It has removed all barriers between those who create content and those who consume it.

And best of all, it has made many of these activities absolutely free! Thanks to the Internet, many of the things artists do now cost nothing. Granted, many things still do cost money (as discussed above). But guess what? For the things that still have a price tag, the Internet has also given artists methods to get the capital they need. One method is known as crowdfunding.

Crowdfunding refers to funding a project by raising contributions from a large group of people. Basically, an artist asks their fans for donations for a specific creative endeavor and, once they get the donations, they use the money to make the endeavor happen. Musicians can use crowdfunding techniques to get donations from their fans and bring their projects to fruition. Crowdfunding has become a very effective tool for artists in recent years. However, if you want to get technical, musicians have actually been "crowdfunding" for centuries in the sense that this practice bears some similarities with the old patron-based systems for creating artistic projects. But thanks to the Internet, artists can use crowdfunding websites like Kickstarter, GoFundMe, Indiegogo, or Patreon to attain a whole new level of success with their fan-funded projects.

Crowdfunding has other benefits for artists on top of the money they receive. A well-executed campaign can have significant promotional value and bring artists a lot more fans. Moreover, a successful campaign guarantees the artist a base of consumers ready to buy the resulting project once it is done. So, not only does crowdfunding provide the capital for an endeavor, a successful crowdfunding campaign can also take away the artist's stress and worry about whether anyone will buy the finished product.

Creating an effective crowdfunding campaign for your project is a project in itself. It takes a lot of work and research to do one well. After all, you are asking people for money, and people won't part with their hard-earned dollars unless you make a great pitch.

Can You Spare a Digital Dime?

Much has been written about the ethics of Internet crowdfunding. Despite its increase in popularity, many artists (including some with whom I work) refuse to engage in this practice. Some take issue with charging people for something that has not been created yet. Others feel queasy about "hitting fans up for money." In addition, some artists and fans alike have complained about the recent rise in prominent artists who are now crowdfunding projects despite presumably having enough personal wealth to self-fund them. To quote an artist colleague of mine: "It is one thing if someone is working as a waitress and can't afford to make their first album. But I feel like many of the people who crowdfund are people who can afford to make their own record. It is dishonest."

Reasonable people can disagree as to the morality of crowdfunding for those who can afford to self-fund. But for artists who lack necessary capital and are trying to launch their careers, I think there is nothing wrong with the practice. Crowdfunding on the Internet is neither cyberbegging nor 21st-century panhandling. Instead, it is an innovative way to allow your fans to play a role in your success and help someone they love create new things. Moreover, crowdfunding is not charity. Your supporters are getting something for their money. In a typical crowdfunding scenario, contributors are given "rewards" for funding your project. The most typical reward is a piece of whatever thing they are helping to fund (e.g, a copy of your album, or a ticket to the show on your tour). And if they make a bigger contribution, you will likely give them additional rewards (e.g., a T-shirt, a personal "thank you" message, or perhaps even a private concert at their home).

Kickstarter, Generally

Though there are many crowdfunding websites out there, we will focus on Kickstarter since it is currently the most popular site for funding creative projects. Launched in 2009, Kickstarter's fundraising platform has helped thousands of musicians, filmmakers, inventors, game designers, and other artistic professionals obtain much-needed capital for their initiatives. According to Kickstarter's website, over nine million people have pledged nearly $2 billion to fund over 250,000 projects on the platform! With Kickstarter, each project gets its own web page on the platform. The page provides the basic information about the project (along with a video by the project creator describing the project) and gives people a way to donate funding to the project via credit card.

Here are some of the basic aspects of using Kickstarter:

- First, it is important to get familiar with the site's lingo. The thing you are trying to fund is known as a "project." You (the person creating the project) are a "creator." Your donors are called "backers." The donations are referred to as "pledges."
- You must propose a specific project for which you are seeking funding. For example, you can't just ask for donations to support your career generally. Instead, you must have a specific thing that will be funded with your backers' pledges, such as an album of songs.
- Kickstarter requires that you post a "funding goal" for your project's page. You must specify the amount of money you will need from your backers to complete all aspects of your

project. The site employs an "all-or-nothing" funding model: If you do not reach your funding goal by the end of your campaign (which can last for up to sixty days), then you receive none of the money pledged by your backers. This model is designed to motivate you (and your backers) to spread the word about your project and get it fully funded.

- As a creator, you will provide prizes ("rewards") to backers who reach certain pledging thresholds for your project. You set the rewards however you like. For a small pledge (like $1) the "reward" might be a simple "thank you" email. For a larger pledge of $10, you might send them a digital download of the record. For pledges in the triple or quadruple digits, you *really* have to be generous (and creative) with your rewards (e.g., credits in the liner notes, autographed stuff, one-on-one music lessons, or private concerts).

- If your project is successfully funded, Kickstarter gets a 5% cut of all funds raised.

Setting Your Funding Goal

Setting your funding goal for your Kickstarter campaign takes a lot of planning. It is critical that you crunch your numbers well. If you set your funding goal too high, you might miss the target and end up with nothing. This would certainly be an undesirable outcome. But the real nightmare scenario is if you set your goal too *low*. If that happens, you might meet it and end up on the hook for a project that you cannot afford to complete.

The first step to setting a proper funding goal is determining the budget for whatever it is that you are creating. Do your research and make sure that you have planned out every single expense. If you are making a record, shop around and get different rates for recording studios and other required personnel (musicians, engineer, mastering house, producer, and others). Talk to other musicians and get some cost ideas from them.

Next, you must determine the other expenses for your project. You must factor in the cost of creating your rewards and disseminating them to your backers. These expenses can be substantial, particularly if you are shipping a lot of goods or offering private concerts that require you to travel. You also want to include the cost of making your Kickstarter video, so you can get your money back for that expense. You also need to tack Kickstarter's 5% fee onto your funding goal, along with another 3-5% to cover credit card processing fees. On top of all of that, you should also strongly consider adding an extra 10% "cushion" to cover unforeseen expenses.

To boil it all down to a simple equation:

<u>Your Kickstarter Funding Goal</u> = Project Budget + Cost of Creating and Shipping Your Rewards + Cost of Kickstarter Video + 5% for Credit Card Processing + 10% Cushion + 5% Kickstarter Fee.

Once their funding goal is set, many creators like to include "stretch goals" to their campaign. Stretch goals are funding targets above and beyond the original funding goal. If you fail to meet a stretch goal, you still get your backers' pledges (provided that the original goal is met). However, if you do meet the stretch goal, you must augment your base project with whatever you identified the stretch funds as being earmarked for (such as additional tracks to your album or creating a bonus music video). Stretch goals can motivate your backers to "run up the score" on a successfully-funded project, getting you more dollars. But stretch goals can also make your project more complicated. If you want to keep your project simple, or if your budget has a lot of unpredictable elements, then you are better off just sticking with your one funding goal.

Rewards

Some people will make pledges in support of your project solely because they love you and they want to see your creation come to life. But most backers are in it to get cool stuff from you. Good rewards can make the difference between your campaign's success and failure. Here are some best practices to create and execute your rewards effectively:

- One of your rewards should always be a "piece of the project." If you are making a recording, backers who donate a modest sum should get a copy of that recording as a reward.
- Have rewards for small pledges and big pledges alike. Don't leave any of your backers out in the cold.
- Shipping costs can add up, so try to favor non-physical rewards over physical ones when possible. One way to accomplish this is to offer a downloadable copy of a recording instead of a CD (unless you want to make a CD version available to those who pledge higher amounts). Other popular non-physical rewards include phone/Skype calls from the artist, a mention in the liner notes, an invitation to an exclusive Google+ hangout with the artist, or an invitation to a private party hosted in the artist's hometown.
- Offer unique rewards. Special rewards will excite your fans and encourage pledges. Copies of your recording or tickets to your show are nice offerings, but unique experiences are what attract bigger backers. Consider offering "collaborative rewards" that let people be a part of your project creation experience. If you are recording music, offer an invitation to your recording session (or better yet, offer an opportunity for someone to play on your record). If you are making a music video, give people the opportunity to be an extra in it.
- Build rewards around your talents. If you are good at doing something (even if it is non-music related), turn that into reward. Doing this will lead to unique rewards that are easy for you to create. Almost any talent can be made into a reward. If you are a good visual artist, offer backers a personalized drawing as one of your rewards. One of my musician friends, who also happens to be an experienced hairstylist, offered a styling session at her house as a Kickstarter reward. Her fans loved it!
- Set practical limits on your rewards so that you can maintain your budget, as well as your sanity. If you are offering rewards that require you to travel (such as a private live performance), make sure you restrict the reward to a

sensible geographic area (e.g., the region surrounding your hometown). You should also offer a finite number of offerings for most of your rewards so that you don't stretch yourself too thin. Finally, avoid rewards that require you to do something on a specific future date down the road. It is hard to predict what your schedule will look like in the future and you don't want to attach yourself to a fixed commitment on a particular day. Many artists have regretted offering a "phone call on your birthday" reward for this reason.

When creating rewards for your Kickstarter campaign, it is vital that you (1) have interesting offerings and (2) price those offerings well. To help you achieve both of those goals, here is a list of rewards inspired by other musicians' Kickstarter campaigns.

The rewards are sorted by pledge level. Though this list can be a useful guide, it should not be taken as gospel. Consider your own personal circumstances, time constraints, and financial situation when devising and pricing your rewards.

Note: Rewards with an asterisk "" denote that any travel expenses are included in the reward. Otherwise, the backer would pay for the accompanying travel costs (either for the backer or for the artist depending on the reward) separately.*

$5 - A "thank you" email

$5 - The backer's name listed on the "Thank You page of the artist's website

$10 - A set of band stickers

$10 - Digital copy of album

$15 - Booklet with information about the artist and pictures

$15 - Album download and artist greeting cards

$20 - Embroidered artist logo patch

$25 - Physical copy of album with handwritten "thank you" note

---

$30 – Physical copy of album and artist poster

$30 – Signed copy of album

$35 – Physical copy of album, digital copy of album, and handwritten "thank you" postcard

$35 – A signed, handwritten lyric sheet of one of the artist's songs

$40 – A "backers only" T-shirt

$40 – A calendar featuring pictures of the artist

$45 – A personalized "thank you" note on the backer's Facebook wall

$50 – A copy of the album and copies of two e-book novels written by the artist

$50 – Tickets to record release party/listening party

$50 – Signed album and signed poster

$50 – Signed album and the artist will record your voicemail message

$50 – Backer's name in the album's liner notes

$70 – A pair of mittens personally knitted by the artist and a signed album

$75 – A signed poster and a signed original art print

$75 – Two tickets to the artist's show

$90 – One of the bow ties the artist wore during their tour

$100 – Two tickets to the artist's show and the after-party

$100 – Skype session with the artist

$125 – Copy of album, artist T-shirt, and autographed posters

$200 – A personalized cello song written and recorded for the backer

$250 – Private online concert by the artist

$250 – One-hour music lesson over Skype with the artist

$300 - Web design services

$350 - Coffee/tea with the artist in the artist's hometown

$400 - Visit to the studio for one day to see the record get made

$500 - Gold bracelet designed by the artist

$500 - Appear as an extra in the artist's music video

$500 - Personalized "thank you" video and autographed CDs and posters

$500 - A home-cooked meal at the artist's house

$750 - Two tickets to a show, meet-and-greet access, access to sound check, and a personalized song dedication

$1,000 - The actual instrument the artist used to make her album (autographed)

$1,000 - Private party performance by solo artist (limited to within 100 miles of artist's hometown)*

$1,500 - Private party performance by solo artist (limited to artist's region)*

$2,500 - Private party performance by solo artist (anywhere in continental United States)*

$5,000 - Private party performance by band (anywhere in continental United States)*

$6,000 - Private party performance by band (anywhere in continental United States)* and executive producer credit on the album

A Successful Kickstarter Campaign

A Kickstarter campaign is a high-stakes, feast-or-famine proposition. From the moment you launch your campaign, you are in a race against the clock. And if you fail to reach your funding goal in time, then you get none of the money donated by your backers. An effective, well-executed campaign can make the difference between receiving full funding for your project and walking away empty-handed.

The first step to a successful campaign is having a sufficient base of potential backers for your project goal. You should not attempt a crowdfunding initiative until you at least have a reasonable number of fans. You need a core group of supporters who will initially back your project and spread the word to their friends. Crowdfunding a project is not Step 1 in an artist-entrepreneur's career. You need to build your entertainment organization a bit first. Establish a presence on YouTube and social media. Amass a strong following of people that will be excited to hear a new musical project from you, and a successful crowdfunding campaign will be much more likely.

Next, your Kickstarter page must effectively describe your project. To accomplish this goal, you need a great video. In fact, one of the most important videos you will ever make as an artist-entrepreneur is your Kickstarter video. If you are ever going to invest a lot of resources into any video, this should be the one. The video will be first thing most backers will view when they see your page, and an engaging one can help you get a lot more donations. Make sure it is well edited with clear audio. A good sample of your music should appear in the video. Use the video to introduce yourself, clearly outline the major aspects of your project, and encourage people to become a backer. Let your passion for your work shine through in your video, and people will feed off of that passion.

The description of your project in your Kickstarter page needs to have a strong pitch. In the end, you are asking people for their money. You are selling something and you need to sell well. Tell people about who you are, what you have done in your career, what specifically you are trying to create, and why they should be interested in that creation (when selling, it always pays to focus on speaking about the things that your buyer wants, as opposed to talking about things that you want). And, of course, be sure to mention the rewards you are offering.

Finally, once your page is up and running, you must promote the heck out of it. Use every possible means of communication at your disposal to share your project with others. This includes posting about your campaign to social media and reaching out to the people on your email list. Provide links to your

Kickstarter page and ask people to back your project. If you have particularly close relationships with certain "Three Fs" people in your life, you should reach out to them directly with personal messages to encourage their support. Your biggest backers will likely be those closest to you; be sure to directly contact those friends, family, and fans with whom you share the tightest bond. Pitch press outlets about your campaign as well if possible.

In your promotional activities, don't just bring up your campaign a single time and move on. Post, email, and tell people about your campaign repeatedly throughout the funding period. Give people constant updates on your campaign's progress, and maintain a sense of excitement about the support you're receiving. People will often need to hear about your project several times before they feel compelled to support you.

Merchandising

A well-executed online crowdfunding campaign is a great way to get your projects off the ground. It can help you finance big-ticket undertakings before you have the money to self-fund them. But crowdfunding is not the only way to raise money. One should certainly not forget about a tried-and-true method that musicians have used for generations to fund their careers: selling merchandise.

Crowdfunding websites like Kickstarter will play a vital role for years to come in helping artists achieve success independently. But there is definitely still a place in your fundraising operation for the time-honored practice of "selling merch." Artists who succeed in the new music industry will be the ones who maximize their revenue streams. Your fans want to be able to get more things from you than just recordings and concert tickets. They want good merchandise too.

A World of Consumers at Your Fingertips

At the risk of sounding like a broken record, effective merchandising is yet another once-expensive music business activity that the Internet has put within the reach of independent artists. Before the music industry found its way to cyberspace, it was impossible for most musicians to sell physical items on a wide scale. Mass merchandising in the old industry required dealing with the

199

burdens of supply chain economics. It meant working with goods distributors and brick-and-mortar retail stores. It meant making significant volume investments. After all, if you want to sell merchandise to the world, you must have enough inventory to reach stores worldwide. It also meant bearing the cost of unsold items. If your merch didn't sell, you had to "eat" the inventory. Obviously, this would be too tall of an order for an independent musician with a limited budget.

Thus, indie artist merchandising in the old days was limited to small-scale retailing activities, like selling a few T-shirts in the parking lot after a gig. This sort of activity could make an artist a few shekels, but that's about all it could do. One simply cannot create a substantive revenue stream when dealing in limited quantities to a tiny pool of consumers.

But the Internet has changed all of that. Today, any artist can create an online storefront to sell their merchandise. Instead of only offering your wares to whomever sticks around after a show, now the entire world is your customer base. Online retailing and worldwide shipping has replaced the traditional supply chain. The Internet (including your own artist website, Bandcamp page, and social media pages) are the new storefronts. You can sell to anyone in the world directly, cutting out all of the distributing and retailing middle men. You can even find websites that will manufacture typical musician merchandise (e.g., t-shirts, stickers, and posters) with your logo for a reasonable cost.

Print-on-Demand Merchandising

In the old world of merchandising, a big challenge for early-career musicians was the need to buy inventory in bulk. For example, if an artist wanted to sell some custom T-shirts, most printers would require that the artist bought the shirts in a large quantity from them (and, even if not, the price per unit was often uneconomical without a bulk order). This is a scary proposition for someone who is just starting out. It can be hard to find the funds to make such a purchase. And if the artist only manages to sell a few units (a likely scenario early in one's career), then they would have to bear the cost of their unsold inventory. It is hard to have a profitable merchandising operation under those circumstances.

200

But online merchandising has changed all of that. Today, musicians have the option of selling merch using "print-on-demand" websites in lieu of maintaining inventory. Instead of bulk buying, an artist can sell shirts and other items on a web platform like CafePress, SpreadShirt, or Zazzle. These sites will print a wide variety of custom merchandise and allow your consumers to buy those items from their platform. Each individual item is manufactured upon the consumer's purchase, meaning that you do not have to buy bulk inventory. With no up-front investment required, you can earn a profit from the very first shirt/hat/coffee mug sold.

The drawback to the print-on-demand model is that it thins out your profit margin. With an on-demand site, you will make money from sale #1, but your *per-sale* profit will be lower than if you bought bulk inventory. If you want the convenience of on-demand merchandising, it will cost you more per unit.

The lesson to be learned here is that print-on-demand websites are a great way to sell merchandise to the world in the early stages of your career. But once you start making some money and have built a reliable fan base, then you are better off buying some inventory. Bulk buying can reduce your per-unit costs by as much as 35% (and sometimes more). Once you are ready to leave on-demand sales behind, there are plenty of websites out there who will mass-produce your inventory for you. CafePress and Zazzle also offer this service, but there are countless other sites that do as well. Shop around cyberspace and find the best deal.

Find Your Unique Merchandising Voice

When conceiving of your own merchandising operation, you might be wondering what items you should sell. Obviously, the standard musician merch staples come to mind: clothing, stickers, posters, and buttons. There's a lot to love about these items. They have had a place in the industry for generations, and there are plenty of websites out there that can make these items for you affordably.

But the artist-entrepreneurs who have the most success in the merchandising game are the ones who think outside the box. They are the ones who supplement the basic merch offerings with a few unique items. Sure, you can always get a nice shirt or poster from these folks, but they will also have some more distinctive things for sale. These special items help the artist distinguish themselves from other performers and foster a deeper connection with their fans.

One type of unique merchandise that fans love is anything that the artist is uniquely able to make. For example, on top of being a marvelous singer and songwriter, indie artist Mary Jennings also makes bolo ties as a hobby. She sells her creations as merchandise to her fans on Etsy, a website for selling handmade items. Not only do her bolo tie sales help her fund her projects, Jennings also notes that they help build fan interest: "I make bolo ties. And people will be like, 'Oh, that's kinda weird. Ok, I'm intrigued.' It is something unique about me that helps me cut through the noise." Jennings' lesson is a valuable one: If you are good at creating something (other than music), sell that something as merchandise. It can help increase your income as well as show music fans what makes you unique. I have seen musicians make and sell bolo ties, paintings, sculptures, jewelry, dolls, books of poetry, scarves, and much more.

Another approach to selling unique merchandise is to offer items that appeal to the specific characteristics of your audience. Every fan base is different. Adopting a one-size-fits-all approach to merchandising prevents you from selling items that will resonate with your devotees. For example, if your music attracts listeners who enjoy partying, then selling items such as custom shot glasses or drink coasters might not be a bad idea. Whatever your fans' attributes, you can boost your sales by offering merchandise that resonates with who your fans are.

CHAPTER 15

OTHER ASPECTS OF YOUR ORGANIZATION

This final chapter will discuss additional components of your entertainment operation. These administrative areas do not fit neatly into any of the previous chapters, but they are exceedingly important. Moreover, these areas tend to be ones where musicians lack knowledge because they involve a lot of specialized concepts. Learning how to navigate these aspects of your organization is critical to achieving, and holding onto, success.

Legal Matters

Presiding over your entertainment empire will force you to confront a wide range of legal issues. This book has already discussed many events in your career that involve legal elements. The first six chapters outlined the legal aspects of record agreements and why these deals are often destructive for artists. Chapter 9 stressed the importance of holding onto the legal rights to your intellectual property. Chapter 11 discussed producer and engineer agreements, full-service distribution contracts, publishing administration deals, and how to register copyrights in your songs and sound recordings. All of these legal subjects play an important role in your entertainment organization.

In addition to the legal issues above, there are some others of which you should be mindful:

Band Agreements and Split Sheets

Many of your best musical creations will result from collaborating with other artists. You will likely perform and record with other musicians throughout your career. Moreover, you might co-write songs with multiple writers. When working with other creative types, you will be well-served by having contracts that articulate everyone's rights and responsibilities (and for everyone to understand these rights and responsibilities at the outset). While it might seem uncool to bring ink and paper into your creative collaborations, getting important details in writing now can prevent litigation later. Contracts might be lame, but nothing is lamer than legal complaints, motions, depositions, and the insides of courtrooms. By handling a tiny amount of business activity up front, you can save yourself a world of stress down the road.

If you carry on any of your music activities with a band, it is important to set up a "Band Agreement" early on. The band agreement will outline everyone's rights and prevent band disputes in the future. Many an expensive band lawsuit could have been avoided if the members took a little bit of time in the early going and sketched out an agreement which covered the following:

- How is money handled? How is income (including record, merchandise, and performance income) distributed? How are expenses funded?
- Who owns the rights to the band name/logo?
- What responsibilities does each band member have? How is labor divided?
- How are band decisions made? Majority rule? Unanimous? Perhaps certain band members get to make decisions in certain areas of operation. Perhaps the band will differentiate between how "creative" and "business" decisions are made in this regard.
- The extent to which band members are allowed to engage in musical or other creative projects outside of the band.
- Who has the authority to actually enter into agreements on the band's behalf?
- What happens if someone leaves the band or the band breaks up? How are assets divided? Who gets to use the band name/logo? What rights will each individual member have regarding the sound recording and compositions the band created?
- What happens if a new member joins the band?
- Who owns the equipment that the band uses?
- How is ownership of the band's sound recordings and musical compositions divided? How is publishing income divided?
- Mediation/arbitration procedures in the event of a legal dispute (it is generally smarter and less expensive to require

the band members to settle their differences out of court in lieu of suing each other).

Another important legal document to employ with your fellow artists is a "Split Sheet." If you co-write a song with other artists, creating and executing a split sheet is critical. A split sheet indicates how the writers will divide ownership of that song. It is a contract that all of the writers will sign. Split sheets will help prevent disputes between the songwriters over royalties and ownership rights. Ideally, the writers should work out the details of the split sheet before any of them exploit the song in any way. At a minimum, a split sheet should include the following elements:

- The title of the song
- The date the song was written
- The names, addresses, birthdates, and phone numbers of the writers
- Each writer's performance rights society (e.g., ASCAP, BMI, or SESAC)
- If any third party is entitled to a percentage of a particular writer's publishing (such as a co-publisher), those third parties and their publishing percentages should be listed
- Each writer's percentage ownership of the song's lyrics
- Each writer's percentage ownership of the song's music
- And, finally, each writer's signature and the date it was signed (an unexecuted agreement isn't worth much)

Also, if a paper split sheet seems a little old-fashioned to you, there are online programs your songwriting team can use to divvy up ownership. SongSplits is a free online service that writers can use to manage their works digitally.

Trademarks

To be able to sell your music, merchandise, and other entertainment endeavors effectively, you need to protect your brand. As you run your entertainment operation, you will use your artist name, logo, and other words and designs to identify your unique products and services. When consumers see your distinctive "marks" on things like recordings, posters, and clothing, you will want them to be assured that these items are coming from you. If someone else were to use these identifiers on similar items, people might get confused and the value of your brand will diminish.

To protect against such an outcome, you must employ the protections provided by federal trademark law. Trademark law gives exclusive rights to trademark holders to use distinctive words and designs that consumers associate with their products. Only the trademark holder can use their trademark in commerce. For example, the "Coca-Cola" brand name and Nike's "swoosh" symbol are both trademarks of their respective companies. The law prevents others from creating a soda product with a confusingly-similar name (or logo) to Coca-Cola, or an athletic apparel company that too closely resembles Nike's logo (or name).

As an independent artist-entrepreneur, you will have some brand identifiers (such as your logos or a professional name) worth protecting with the force of law. To do this, you must pursue valid trademarks in your distinctive brand words and images. Trademark law is quite complicated. Thus, a comprehensive discussion of the subject is beyond the scope of this book. However, artists should know some of the basics:

- Generally, whoever first uses a mark in a particular goods and services area gets the rights to the mark in that area. Therefore, before using a particular artist name or image as a mark, make sure that no other artists are using it already.

- The more distinctive your mark, the stronger the protection (and also the less likely that someone else is using your mark). When it comes to word marks for artists, words that are completely made-up (like Lexus or Häagen-Dazs) or at least are not associated with music tend to be stronger than descriptive words related to one's industry (while you might like "meta" names, if you name your group "Band," you will find it exceedingly difficult to get trademark protection).

- Trademark rights mainly extend to the categories of goods and services for which the mark is used. As a result, the strength of one's mark is much weaker in other categories (unless the mark is incredibly famous). For example, if your

206

professional name in music is Red Bird and you have a valid mark in that name, you will likely be able to prevent other artists from using that name. However, you won't be as successful at stopping an auto insurance company from using Red Bird as its name.

- To afford maximum protection for a trademark, formally register the mark with the United States Patent and Trademark Office. Technically, trademark rights exist from the moment that the trademark holder begins using the mark in commerce. However, formal government registration gives the trademark holder additional valuable rights. For one thing, registering a mark endows it with nationwide protection. Without registration, one's mark only has protection in the geographic areas where the mark is actually used in commerce. Moreover, much like in the realm of copyright, government registration provides a trademark with a legal presumption of the mark's validity.

- When registering a trademark, the applicant will select the international goods and services classes in which the mark in question is used. For musicians, these classes can include (but are not limited to) sound recordings (Class 9), posters and other promotional materials (Class 16), clothing and apparel (Class 25), and artist performances (Class 41).

Trademark registration can be done online at the Patent and Trademark Office website (uspto.gov). Online registration costs $275 per mark per class. I _strongly_ recommend using an attorney to register your marks. Trademark registration is far less user-friendly than copyright registration. The forms are confusing and it is easy to make a mistake. Moreover, a lawyer can review your unique situation and advise you on (1) whether your mark is available for registration and (2) the classes in which you should register your mark.

Legal Entity Formation

Now let's focus a bit on the "entrepreneur" half of the "artist-entrepreneur" title that this book bestows upon you. If your career progresses as you and I hope it will, then your creative activities will start to generate money. Because your goal is not just to entertain people, and you are trying to run a business, you need to formally separate your business activities from your personal world. To do this, you must set up a legal entity for your entertainment career.

When you start engaging in your music business activities, the law provides a default legal structure for you. If you are doing business by yourself, you are a "sole proprietor," entitled to all profits of your business. If you are doing business with a group of people (such as a band) and splitting the profits, the law would deem that a "partnership," with each partner entitled to an equal share of the profits (in the absence of an agreement saying otherwise). You receive these two business statuses without any formal government action. It is simply the legal structure you get if you don't set up anything else.

And in your career's infancy, you might get by just fine with this arrangement. However, once your entertainment activities start generating not-insubstantial amounts of income, you should start conducting those activities with a more legitimate legal entity—such as an Limited Liability Company (LLC) or an S-Corporation. Forming such an entity can make your life much easier come tax time. It is generally easier to track profits and write off losses with an LLC/S-Corp than it is as a sole proprietor or partnership.

But the most compelling reason to run your business through a formal entity is to protect your finances. Creating these entities costs a little bit of money (somewhere in the hundred-dollar range annually, though it will vary depending on the state where you incorporate), but it can save you a lot more down the road. Sole proprietorships and partnerships are "unlimited liability" entities. This means that you (and your personal assets) are on the hook for the debts of your business. Moreover, if someone sues your sole proprietorship, they can go after your business bank account and your personal wealth and possessions.

With unlimited liability, debts and lawsuits can not only ruin your entertainment career—they can ruin your life. Conversely, entities like LLCs and S-Corps offer "limited liability," crafting a wall of separation between your business assets and your personal assets. When your LLC owes debts or gets sued (as the case may be), only the LLC's assets are at risk (generally). The things you personally own have a greater chance of remaining safe.

To maintain your limited liability, it is critical that you do not mix your personal activities with your business activities. Have a separate bank account for your entity that employs its own checks and credit/debit cards. Do not pay for personal items out of your business account (and vice versa). Make sure all entertainment contracts you sign list your entity (and not you) as the contracting party. If a court cannot determine where your entertainment career ends and you begin, you could have a harder time protecting your personal assets if something bad happens.

In fact, when your entertainment operation reaches a high level of sophistication, you might consider creating multiple legal entities to separate each of your industry activities. That way, you can protect each of your units from the creditors of one particular unit. For example, I have one client who has separate entities for his recording, song publishing, touring, and merchandising activities.

Creating a legal entity for your entertainment career has considerable benefits, but it also presents a host of tax issues. Be sure to enlist the services of an accountant to help you set up and administer these companies.

A Final Note Regarding Legal Issues

I want to close this section by reiterating a point I have discussed throughout this book: Please consult an attorney when confronting legal issues. Perhaps there are some legal-ish tasks that you can do without a lawyer (like registering a basic copyright or signing a very short and simple contract), but you should have a lawyer help you with anything beyond that. Legal matters involving contracts, trademark registrations, and forming and maintaining your entities are almost always more complicated than they seem. Without the guidance of counsel, it is easy to inadvertently give up a valuable right or obligate yourself to something beyond your capability.

Believe me, I know hiring a lawyer can be expensive. However, it can be far more expensive to *not* hire one. If you pay a lawyer to fix a bad contract before you sign it, the legal fees will be manageable. But if you forego legal assistance until that bad contract stalls out your career or puts you in a courtroom, those fees will be much worse, and it could very well be too late to save your career. The earlier you get an attorney involved in your career, the cheaper your legal fees.

Besides, if you are resourceful, there are plenty of ways for you to find affordable counsel. Look for entertainment lawyers within your Three Fs, or ask other musicians for a referral. If you are indigent, you can also reach out to a VLA (Volunteer Lawyers for the Arts) organization in your area for pro bono assistance.

Managers

A manager is someone that an artist hires to help them run the various aspects of their career. Ideally, this person should be an experienced music and business professional who is strongly committed to achieving the artist's goals. Good managers can help an artist keep their entertainment operation running smoothly, which in turn allows the artist to run their career effectively.

Managers work with the relevant personnel in each sector of the artist's operation (e.g., promotion, songwriting, recording, fundraising, merchandising, live performances, and non-music business projects) to keep things on track for their client. In exchange for their services, a manager will usually receive a percentage of the artist's entertainment revenue (usually in the 15% range)—though some managers will work on a straight salary.

Do You Need a Manager?

In my legal practice, artists have occasionally approached me seeking advice on getting a good manager. Some of them even asked me if I could refer them to someone. When I ask them why they are in the market for a manager, I usually receive a response along the lines of: "I want someone who can guide my career. Preferably, it should be someone who knows the industry and can help me get gigs and other opportunities. I am hoping that a manger can take my music to the next level and make me a star."

These words are indicative of what many young artists envision the role of a manager to be. After all, it resembles what managers look like in most made-for-TV movies about the music business. We've all seen these flicks. They usually involve some

210

savvy entertainment mogul who discovers a lovely unknown vocalist singing in a dingy club in front of half a dozen people. The mogul, realizing this vocalist's talent, pulls her aside in the club, tells her "You don't belong here; you're a star," and then proceeds to guide her to the top of the industry over the next hour-and-a-half.

Sorry, folks. It does not work that way. Movies portray managers in this fashion because what managers actually do would make for a really boring movie. No one wants to see ninety minutes of someone reviewing documents, having tedious calls with publicists and lawyers, and drinking eleven cups of coffee a day. When artists come to me envisioning this Hollywood-ized view of artist managers, I feel compelled to set them straight so that they can understand the real purpose behind hiring a manager. I begin by laying down a few truths:

1. It is NOT a Manager's Job to Make You Famous

A manager does not make you a star. *You* make you a star. A manager simply helps you manage your stardom. Granted, managers can be a valuable resource as you advance in your career. They can provide sage counsel in helping you to maximize your fame. But, ultimately, you are responsible for creating your own success.

If someone offers to manage you and says that they can "take you to the top," be very wary. For one thing, the manager's definition of "the top" will likely involve trying to find you a record deal or even signing you to a record label that they own. Either way, after reading through this book, you are now more than aware that you do not want any part of that. You should not be interested in giving 15% of your entertainment revenues to a manager just so that they can sign you to a label that will take 30% of your entertainment revenues (along with your record royalties and your master rights).

Moreover, any manager offering you a shortcut up the mountain will likely expect too much from you in return, and they will almost assuredly under deliver on their guarantee. I have encountered many artists who signed deals with managers who promised them the world. These managers—who were often prominent figures in the industry—would demand their clients give them sizable portions of their income and full control over their careers. In exchange for these valuable assets, the artists would rarely experience any significant professional advancement. In fact, they were frequently worse off than they were previously because the money they used to make is now in the manager's pocket.

2. It is NOT a Manager's Job to Find You Gigs

Some artists want a manager because they think such a person can book more and better gigs for them. I can certainly understand why an artist might desire someone who can fill these needs. Live performances remain a viable income opportunity for musicians even as recorded music revenues continue to shrink across the industry.

However, the notion that managers can book gigs for artists is one of the most pervasive misconceptions that musicians have. Let me be crystal clear: Managers do <u>not</u> get you gigs. That is the job of a booking agent. In fact, it is illegal in many states (including California) to work as a booking agent unless one is properly licensed and adheres to strict regulations. Many managers have been forced by courts to disgorge their commissions after booking gigs without a license. So if a manager tries to get you to sign with them by making promises of employment, this person does not understand the basic laws affecting their profession. Thus, you should avoid these managers like the plague.

3. You Probably Don't Need a Manager...Yet

When artists approach me asking for help finding a manager, my first impulse is to congratulate them and give them a high five. "How cool!" I think to myself. "This person is doing very well. After all, they must have a really impressive career if they need to hire someone else to help them run it." Most of the time, however, I am mistaken. All too often the artist talking to me is still getting their career off the ground, but still seems to think they need someone to manage their lemonade stand of an entertainment operation.

If you are in the initial stages of your entertainment career, don't waste your limited resources on a manager. You don't need a manager in the early going because you already have one: You. You are more than capable of running your entertainment operation when you start out. In fact, many artist-entrepreneurs continue to manage themselves even after they become established, as they (often rightfully) believe that no one is better suited to run their organization than they are.

You do not need a manager unless you are better off having someone else administer the day-to-day aspects of your operation. This will not be the case unless your career has truly taken off and there are simply not enough hours in the day for you to actually pull the levers on your own. Until that day comes, there is no reason for you to defer your management control. Therefore, in all but the rarest of circumstances, you are your own best manager.

Management Agreements

Assuming you are in a place where you actually *need* a manager, you will need a contract in place to govern your relationship. As if this has not been repeated throughout this book, I will say it again: Have a lawyer look through any complex agreement (especially a management agreement) before signing anything. That being said, there are a couple provisions you will want to make sure you have in your management contract.

First, both the artist and the manager should be able to end the relationship at any time. A lot of managers will want the contract to have a set term, meaning that they will be your manager for as many years as the contract dictates. You should reject such a setup. The manager works for you. If you don't like the job they are doing, you should be able to show them the door. Similarly, if the manager no longer feels they can work for you, they should be able to walk away. For an artist-manager relationship to thrive, both sides need to trust each other and feel comfortable working together. If one of the two parties no longer feels that way, forcing them to continue the relationship can make things really messy.

Some managers bristle at such an arrangement. They will argue that the contract must have a set term. These folks fear some contrived nightmare scenario in which they help guide the artist into a big payday of some kind, and then the artist immediately fires them to avoid having to pay any future commissions. I tend not be a big believer in this argument. For one thing, if the manager is truly good at their job, the artist will want to keep them around because they value the manager's ability to run their organization and to keep their career moving forward.

But if the manager truly fears losing out on a big opportunity, the answer is not taking away both sides' rights to end the relationship at any time. Instead, the agreement can include some kind of "sunset clause," in which the manager continues to receive some of their commissions for a set period after termination of the contract. That way, the manager can still share in the success they helped foster without ever creating a situation where one side may have to stay in a bad relationship.

Second, the contract must make clear that the artist has the ultimate authority over all aspects of their career. The manager manages the artist's *operation*, but does not manage the artist. The artist should remain free to set his or her general career goals and direction, with the manager helping the artist to accomplish those goals. The artist is the manager's boss—not the other way around.

Granted, for reasons of practicality, there are situations where the artist will want the manager to make decisions for them. The artist should give the manager the authority to take all necessary actions to accomplish the artist's objectives. In fact, it might even be prudent to give the manager the ability to actually execute contracts on the artist's behalf (this is known having "power of attorney") to help the organization run more efficiently. However, the management contract should make clear that the manager will (1) act within the artist's directives when making decisions, (2) keep the artist informed of all business developments, and (3) not exercise his or her power of attorney on any particular contract without the artist's consent.

Accountant/Business Manager

The more money you make in your career, the harder it will be to manage. In the early stages of your entertainment operation, you might be able to handle your own finances if you are good with numbers. In fact, many artists enjoy doing their bookkeeping as it allows them to remain constantly abreast of their financial position. However, the time may come when you need to enlist the services of an accountant/business manager to keep your dollars in order.

An accountant can track and manage your cash flow and also ensure that your taxes are properly filed and paid. Eventually, these activities can become quite complicated for an artist, especially once the artist begins operating under a legal entity and receives income from multiple sources. Once this is the case for you, you will definitely need an accountant. When you are at this point, look for an accountant within your "Three Fs" or seek a referral from another artist. If you already have an accountant doing your personal taxes, they might be willing to do some accounting services for your professional career (such as your quarterly tax preparation) for only a slight increase in their compensation.

Booking Agents

Live performances are a cash cow for most artists' music operations. Not only do artists make money directly for performing live shows, but gigs also bring in cash indirectly in the form of merchandise sales and increased fan engagement. A booking agent can help you find these opportunities. These professionals have strong connections with a wide range of venues and events, and can help you secure gigs both in and out of your region. In exchange for their services, the agent takes a commission, which is set by law in many states and is usually in the neighborhood of ten percent.

However, just because agents exist does not mean you don't need to book gigs for yourself, too. In fact, you will procure most of your early-career show bookings. There are a lot of things you can do to maximize your chances of getting lots of gigs:

- Affiliate with other musicians, combining your resources and booking gigs together as a package deal.
- Network as much as you can. Reach out to venues and promoters. Get to know the bookers at the venues in your area. Be persistent but not pushy.
- Create a professional-looking "booking kit" that you can share with bookers at venues. At a minimum, the kit should include a band bio, photos, copies of your music, and your booking price.

215

- Open for artists who are further along in their career. You can play some great venues and make valuable connections this way.
- Look to your fellow musicians for booking contacts. Offer to exchange contacts with them.
- Let bookers in your area know that you are available to fill in on gigs if other artists cancel.
- Use social media to reach out to your fans for leads on gigs. This can be especially valuable when you are trying to expand your performances to venues outside of your geographic area.

Above all else, the best thing you can do to keep your gigs flowing is to make sure you are putting out a great product. Good networking and a snazzy booking kit can only take you so far if your live show stinks. You need to practice constantly to make your show as tight as possible. Make sure that your performance is visually-engaging as well as pleasant-sounding. Your visual aspect and how you present yourself matters. Also, make sure that you keep your content fresh. It is vitally important to constantly incorporate new material in your shows. If you keep doing the same set list at every gig, then even your die-hards will eventually lose interest in your performances.

Once you gain some traction as a live performer, you can start reaching out to a booking agent to find more opportunities for you. If you already have some decent gigs under your belt and have earned a positive reputation, it will be easier to find an agent in your area willing to take you on. Look for an agent who has particularly strong connections with mid- and large-size venues, festivals, and conventions. You will want an agent who is a member of the National Association of Campus Activities (NACA). These individuals can help you get gigs performing at colleges, which are often quite lucrative and can help you expand your geographic reach.

AFTERWORD

I've been given the honor and privilege of occupying this space, and even more so, the freedom to do so however I wish. As I considered the burden of this awesome responsibility, I initially planned to focus on the relationship I'm truly fortunate to share with your author.

I could tell you about how we met years ago over a clever, poorly timed joke. I could go on about how—depending on the day—we've been friends, classmates, teammates, colleagues, partners, and rivals, too. I could even try my best to describe for you the enormous degree of respect I have for Ryan and how humbling it has been to watch him learn his craft and zealously represent his clients, all without being able to decide which of those things he takes MORE seriously. Unfortunately, however, you don't have time for any of that. So, it'll have to suffice to say, I know this guy and how much he knows his s*** when it comes to this field, and, much more importantly, how much he cares about sharing his message with you.

You're pressed for time for the simple reason that if you're the target market for this book, it's possible that some of its content may have become obsolete while you wondered about that clever, poorly timed joke. That's the honest truth about how quickly this industry is evolving for you as an independent artist. In a way, I don't envy you the task of preparing, sharing, creating, sharing, promoting, sharing, distributing, and sharing your content, but in a different way, I'm desperately jealous of your opportunity to do it.

Every day, the tools necessary for you to reach the world on your own terms become more and more accessible. Put simply, you don't have to allow the evolution of this industry to happen to you. Instead, you can and should actively participate. Sure, there are some pitfalls you're going to want to avoid, and now you're aware of a significant number of them. You've also been presented with a few cool ways to emphasize the *indie* in indie artist. Don't stop here. Read another book, and then another. Share your experiences with your fellow artists. Embrace the opportunity to hear about theirs. If you can keep learning at the rate that you're creating, and I hope you do, my most current device will surely overflow with stuff I'd really like to read, watch and listen to. That's the space I'd really like to occupy.

I bet you think your stuff is pretty good. I bet it is, too. I hope I get to experience it someday, in exactly the way you choose.

-Josh Morales, Esq.

Josh Morales is a corporate and entertainment attorney currently practicing with Parker Poe Adams & Bernstein, LLP in Raleigh, North Carolina.

ABOUT THE AUTHOR

Ryan Kairalla is a lawyer, writer, teacher, and podcaster. Ryan advises clients in the music industry on a wide range of entertainment and business matters including recording agreements, publishing agreements, management agreements, music licensing, media appearances, live performances, entertainment litigation, copyright and trademark counseling, and corporate matters. He has represented chart-topping hitmakers and up-and-coming musicians alike.

Ryan is a graduate of New York University School of Law where he received the Jack J. Katz Memorial Award for Excellence in Entertainment Law. He is also a *summa cum laude* graduate of the University of Miami School of Business. He is licensed to practice in Florida, New York, and California.

He writes frequently on legal subjects, with his work being featured in the *Journal of Intellectual Property and Entertainment Law* and on his *Break the Business* blog. He also hosts the *Break the Business Podcast*, a weekly discussion of entertainment law, independent music, and popular culture.

Ryan is also an education advocate. In addition to his entertainment law practice, Ryan advises education companies in intellectual property law, corporate law, and contract issues. His passion for education is not limited to the legal world, as he also teaches part-time at Doral College in South Florida.

Ryan lives in Miami, Florida.

INDEX